BAD FOR US

Other Books by John Portmann

When Bad Things Happen to Other People

Sex and Heaven: Catholics in Bed and at Prayer

In Defense of Sin (Editor)

Bad for Us

The Lure of Self-Harm

JOHN PORTMANN

BEACON PRESS · BOSTON

BEACON PRESS
25 Beacon Street
Boston, Massachusetts 02108-2892
www.beacon.org

Beacon Press books
are published under the auspices of
the Unitarian Universalist Association of Congregations.

07 06 05 04   8 7 6 5 4 3 2 1

This book is printed on acid-free paper that meets the uncoated
paper ANSI/NISO specifications for permanence as revised in 1992.

Text design by Isaac Tobin
Composition by Wilsted & Taylor Publishing Services

LIBRARY OF CONGRESS CATALOGING-IN-PUBLICATION DATA

Portmann, John.
    Bad for us: the lure of self-harm / John Portmann.
        p. cm.
    Includes bibliographical references and index.
    ISBN 0-8070-1618-7 (cloth : alk. paper)
    1. Self-defeating behavior. I. Title.
BF637.S37P67 2004
155.2—dc22   2003020340

For Dan, naturally

*Twenty years from
now you will be more
disappointed by the
things you didn't do than
by the ones you did.*

*So throw off the bowlines.
Sail away from the safe
harbor. Catch the trade
winds in your sails.
Explore. Dream.*

—MARK TWAIN

In the destructive element immerse.

—JOSEPH CONRAD

contents

preface

Where the Wild Things Are

INTRIGUING STORIES OF SELF-INFLICTED WOUNDS JUMP
out at us from newspapers and television. A self-made media
celebrity gets accused of insider trading (Martha Stewart), a
pillar of virtue is exposed for having gambled away eight million dollars in Las Vegas (William J. Bennett, Jr.), a baseball
hero finds himself ejected from a televised game when umpires
discover cork in his shattered bat (Sammy Sosa), an arch conservative talk show host publicly confesses an addiction to
pain-killers (Rush Limbaugh), and one of the most celebrated
basketball players of the day denies that he sexually assaulted
a nineteen-year-old woman but does admit to misconduct: "I
am disgusted at myself for making the mistake of adultery"
(Kobe Bryant). While one Hollywood star is put on trial for illegal drug use (Robert Downey, Jr.), another is found guilty of
theft (Winona Ryder). The names and faces may change from
year to year, but the drama remains the same: we crash and
burn.

Socially self-destructive impulses are by no means re-
stricted to the rich, famous, or powerful. In 2003 a New Jersey
student graduated first in her high school class but, because
she had taken many of her courses at home, was asked to
share the grand prize with another student. Objecting that
she should be the sole valedictorian, Blair Hornstine sued the
Moorestown school board and won, making herself unpopular
in the process. She skipped graduation amid reports that her
classmates planned to boo her. A few weeks later, Harvard Uni-

versity learned that Hornstine had plagiarized some of the articles she had written for a local newspaper. It quickly rescinded its offer of admission. Why did a school valedictorian on the first rung of the success ladder risk losing it all?

That so many people do what's bad for them fascinates me. There seems to be no end to the harm we can do ourselves. Wild things lurk within us and we must beware them. Watching pornography may be fun, but for most people it's emotionally demoralizing. And so we turn away. Taking more than one husband or more than one wife may strike us as an excellent idea, but for most people it's emotionally exhausting. And so we can't. Self-control, backed in most cases by law, lifts us out of temptation, removing us from a part of ourselves we may come to despise.

Even a short study of what's bad for us would almost have to hinge on when and where we live—on cultural, social, religious, scientific beliefs and prejudices of a given time and place. (Although we'll see that Kant thought the list remained more or less fixed, much like the Ten Commandments.) Almost anywhere in the Western hemisphere, peculiar ideas used to circulate. We used to think it bad for us to live in a society in which people could drink alcohol. A world in which women could vote in political elections or earn university degrees used to scare us. Doctors used to tell us that masturbation would make us blind and that uncharitable thoughts about our neighbors would make us ugly. And so on. This moral menu deserves our attention, and I showcase it in Part One of this book.

Self-control often amounts to another way of saying "good judgment." When it comes to good judgment, the shouting starts. "Pull yourself together," "get it together," "don't lose your cool": We may hear these exhortations when we appear to others to be losing control. Frequently, children are admonished to maintain self-control, lest the world sink into chaos. That's the implicit lesson we take from teachers, parents, judges, priests, bosses, and parole officers.

We know the rules. We sometimes disobey them anyway. What on earth darts through our minds when we press ahead and jump ship? What are we thinking when we do what's bad for us? Why do we choose to rave when it is against our interest? We can find comfort, focus, and inspiration in danger. In Parts II and III of this book I probe the spirit of defiance that animates so many acts of self-harm.

Risk Analysis of Naughtiness

Having fun is a big part of life, for children and adults alike. Breaking rules can be exhilarating, as can surprising others by our unconventional appearance or behavior. Skinny-dipping in public places is usually illegal, but taking an airline flight dressed as a member of the opposite sex is not. Either idea may appeal to thrill-seekers, some of whom will prefer to jump from high bridges while tied to a bungee cord, others of whom will savor the risk of getting caught speeding. Princess Diana allegedly enjoyed dropping into random London drugstores and ostentatiously purchasing early pregnancy tests. To each his or her own.

Having fun sometimes borders on stupidity. An independent American group issues an annual report of gaffes as hilarious as they are disturbing. The Darwin Awards publicize monumental blunders, the mistakes of apparent idiots who do themselves in, only to end up in jail or six feet under.[1] These poor souls proved themselves their own worst enemy. Are they really so different from us? When we amuse ourselves, we sometimes flirt with disaster. On purpose.

We are not supposed to hurt ourselves; we all share a moral responsibility to nurture and honor ourselves. So say moralists from time immemorial. The antidote to sin and dangerous merrymaking is self-control, an elusive blend of continence and delayed gratification. We tend to think of self-control as a duty, and as something we do for our own good.

Duties to the self can become a drag. We occasionally yearn for a break from high moral seriousness. Enter the carnival, which has been raised to an art form since ancient Western harvest festivals. Various forms of carnival were linked to the feasts of the Roman Catholic Church. In addition to saints' days, Christians celebrated the day before Lent (Mardi Gras, Fastnacht). Venetian Carnevale, to take perhaps the most glamorous example, permits, indeed encourages, debauchery before the austere sacrifices mandated by a pious observance of Lent (it is debatable how seriously Italians take the austerity part today). The elaborate masks of Carnevale help relieve the pressure of work, moral expectations, school, marriage, competition, and just being oneself (as well as accountability for our actions). Masks loosen social boundaries and interrupt dreariness. Playfully, the poor pretend to be rich, while the rich step off their comfortable perches. Masks unleash eccentric postures and comic gestures, for the grotesque and the disgusting no longer seem so frightening. Organized naughtiness takes other forms, from the frat house blow-out to the raucous protest march. Gaining in notoriety is Burning Man, a sprawling annual event in the Nevada wilderness. At this weeklong festival, many costumed revelers take the drug Ecstasy.

Accounts of small-scale carnivals or of the jubilation that erupts in them have appeared in many books. In "Epithalamion," for example, the English Jesuit priest-poet Gerard Manley Hopkins describes the euphoria of tearing off one's clothes and diving into the local swimming hole. In this nineteenth-century poem about the voluptuous distraction of swimming, we enter a jubilant celebration of boys laughing in a river lined by a "bushybowered wood." A passing stranger is lured by the happy shouts, finds a pool nearby, strips, and also frolics in the "kindcold element." Carefree boys guiltlessly enjoying the river's fullness find a similar kind of escape as do the revelers at carnival. But even escape into a swimming hole can signal the drama of being swept away. One of the recurrent themes in Hopkins's poems is self-erasure. In one of the "terrible sonnets," he attempts to capture the mystic loss of self and connection to God through nature. Losing the self fascinated him, as it has many religious thinkers.

Laughter must be one of the most common forms of escape. Forces well up inside us and overflow the boundaries of moral seriousness. We take a holiday from severity. An emotional release, laughter can show us the world in its most appealing aspects. And laughing at the past, especially one full of disappointment and embarrassment, can help fend off panic attacks as perhaps nothing else can.

Laughter and mischievous fun underlie a good deal of role-playing. We can find ourselves by trying on different emotional styles for size. I don't mean to recommend pursuing any way of life whatsoever, simply to add to the diversity of our experiences. We must beware of those choices which, in the long run, narrow down or preclude other possibilities, for instance unwanted pregnancy. But through experimentation with escape, we learn to perform a mental calculus of personal danger, a risk analysis of the naughtiness we contemplate.

The Wild Blue Yonder

Hurting someone else is one thing, and hurting ourselves another. An athlete who undermines a competitor's chance to win (think Tonya Harding, the American figure skater, and her soap operatic scheme to make it to the 1994 Olympics) can be disqualified, but an athlete who undermines him or herself through drunken carousing the night before a competition cannot.

What can we get away with all by ourselves? The answer comes down not only to our success at stealth but also the wrath of others. Whatever others dictate is bad for us stands in the way of our private freedom and therefore deserves our careful attention. We can defy popular wisdom, it turns out, but our naughtiness comes at a cost.

Homeopathy, a term familiar from medical care, has much to teach us about living morally. Just as doctors will inject into our bodies small doses of live virus from which we seek protection, so might we taste small samples of naughtiness from time to time in order to contain a dangerous hunger for all-out transgression.

This advice amounts to more than a recommendation for all things in moderation, for this counsel sees intrinsic value in naughtiness. In naughtiness, we experiment with the person we aspire to become. And in naughtiness we decide whether the moral values we're expected to embrace really suit us.

Certainly, we sometimes crave what's downright dangerous. Since Adam and Eve, temptation has crept into and altered individual quests for perfection. In a scenario lamentably familiar to American university administrators, earnest parents drop off well-groomed children at campus at the end of every summer. Within a day or two, the child has consumed a dangerous quantity of alcohol and risked injury and sexual assault through resulting carelessness. Total freedom requires the self-control these young students lack, for want of practice.

All that is verboten comes in particularly handy to those who want to grab attention. The shortest path to fame in a world obsessed with celebrities is through self-destruction, for people find our dramas riveting. Not just daredevils like Harry Houdini and Evel Knievel, but ordinary people may risk the modicum of status, influence, or money they've accumulated. Friends and strangers alike find themselves drawn to the spectacle of our battle against good health, good fortune, or good sense. Because it is unseemly and generally illegal to torture other people, we have only ourselves to offer up. Precisely because we know that most people are driven by self-interest, a raging desire to improve their lot in life, we puzzle over glaring exceptions to this general law of human behavior. Self-destruction can make us famous, and it can make celebrities even more famous than they already are—think of O. J. Simpson holding a gun to his head on the Los Angeles freeway,

Karen Carpenter starving herself to death, and Princess Diana hurling herself down staircases (or so she claimed in Andrew Morton's tell-all book). The downward spiral of another can hold us spellbound, much in the way that the sight of an auto accident can.

At the same time, we admire people wholly committed to a cause. In 1965, the American media covered the shocking death of a young Quaker who protested the Vietnam War by immolating himself in the parking lot below the window of Secretary of Defense Robert McNamara. According to McNamara's biographer, "A column of orange flame lept twelve feet high as the clothes and flesh burned."[2] Like this young American, suicide bombers in the Mideast martyr themselves for a higher purpose. Suicide bombers, unfortunately, will undoubtedly become an American preoccupation in coming years, in part because of the threat they pose and in part for their utter disregard for the cost of this self-expression. It used to be said that each of us carries the seeds of his or her own destruction, and suicide bombers dramatize that point.

No one thinks that suicide bombers enjoy their final act, but some of us secretly suspect that wild parties pit people against themselves in a similar way. At issue is how carefully we protect our sacred self, if at all. The moral problem with wild parties is that those who go in for them accept unnecessary risk. It might be a slippery slope from mixing drugs and alcohol at a party to utter self-destruction, despite the guffaws of ravers. The sober may see a veiled death wish in the wild at heart, and the suicide bomber disturbs anyone who thinks we have a duty to take care of ourselves.

Looking a lot like the suicide bomber is the person who throws him- or herself on an enemy bomb to prevent harm to others, or to protest a war. As the United States worried over an imminent war with Iraq in early 2003, newspapers carried stories of Westerners in Iraq who had pledged to throw themselves on American bombs, in a costly plea for peace. Human shields had popped up in the Persian Gulf War of 1991. After its

1990 invasion of Kuwait, the Iraqis rounded up hundreds of oil workers, bankers, and other expatriates, forcing them to live for months at scores of sites including Iraqi military bases and industrial plants. These shields were eventually released, before the war. The United States warned repeatedly that even though the shields of 2003 were volunteers, their use would still be considered a war crime. "Deploying human shields is not a military strategy, it's murder, a violation of the laws of armed conflict and a crime against humanity, and it will be treated as such," Secretary of Defense Donald Rumsfeld warned.[3] The shields themselves stressed that they had come to protect civilians and not to support the Iraqi government, but the Iraqis perhaps blurred this distinction.

Like human shields, we insist that we are masters of our own fate. We reserve the right to put at risk our bodies, our futures, our reputations. Flirting with disaster can ennoble us. It also toughens our skin, distracts us from our cares, and sometimes relieves stress. Solitary transgressions can lead to exciting breakthroughs. We discover corners of our personality we didn't know existed. We see ourselves in a new light and bask in the thrill. Alas, some of these erotic or spiritual or athletic adventures really can kill us. A disapproving world does us the favor of trying to stop us from going too far. Curiosity killed the cat and could do us in as well. What our parents, teachers, employers, and friends warn is bad for us may, in fact, be bad for us.

Finding our way in the world requires self-control. We must prevent ourselves from the fate of the foolish. Risk analysis can save us from certain doom while preserving the possibility for brash forays into self-discovery. We rely on risk analysis of temptations throughout life, yet guidebooks seem hard to find. The ever-changing set of things labeled "bad for us" differs from the set of things called "what we can get away with." So many of our transgressions are never found out that we almost manage to believe that what we conceal from others isn't really bad for us at all. Harming ourselves, it might seem, comes from getting found out. If this were true, then there wouldn't really be such a thing as self-harm, only the harm others do us when they accuse us of naughtiness.

This book explores the wisdom of what's bad for us. There is a special way of testing our strength we call raving; it can produce a heady rush of feeling alive. Like the rhapsodic dance to which this emotional surge gave its name in the 1990s, raving tempts us to throw over good sense and social constraints. Just take a leap of faith into the future and see where you land, we silently urge ourselves. Raving, like temptation, beckons us. How we will resist and why we should: These questions summon all our mental powers.

Going for It

St. Paul says in Romans 4:15 "where no law is, there is no transgression." In the television series *Seinfeld*, a principal character presses on St. Paul's thinking and, in the process, invites us to question the transparency of what's bad for us. George has sex with the office cleaning lady—on his desk, no less ("The Red Dot," Episode #29). When he later informs her that he has no intention of pursuing a relationship, she reports him. George is puzzled when his boss fires him. "There's no harm in what I've done," he challenges his boss. Recounting the whole story to his friends later on, he insists that if only his boss had informed him that having sex with the cleaning lady in the office was frowned upon, he never would have let himself go.

We may at times find ourselves similarly surprised by the world. In 1998, for example, Harvard University forced the dean of its divinity school to step down after the discovery that the dean had downloaded hundreds of pornographic images onto his hard drive. George's question prompts us to ask how much we really know about what's good for us. This is the question I'll probe in Part One, taking as my guide Immanuel Kant, the most influential moral philosopher of modernity.

Part Two explores magical self-control, the ability to say no to ourselves and prevent the stinging regret George feels on *Seinfeld*. Where does self-control come from and how do we get more of it? When all is said and done, do we really want more of it? Would we be able to harm ourselves in a world in which nothing was bad for us? What would such a world look like? Modern artists such as Matthew Barney help us conceptualize what we can only see through a glass darkly. Contemporary art has taken a decidedly transgressive, in-your-face turn, much as contemporary music and comedy have done. Whereas religious thinkers and social conservatives tend to assume that the whole notion of what is bad for us is patently obvious, artists and comedians undermine this view. Determining what's bad for us used to be the job of the censor or the mullah, not the artist. Today, though, the artist inspires us to question the censor, who cannot satisfy us much longer with treacly platitudes (for example, "Evil is bad" and "Virtue is good"). Although this is certainly not a book about Matthew Barney, adventurers like Barney who "go for it" show us the cost of self-control: We who keep our feet on the ground may end up feeling trapped in drab little lives. Is that the best we can hope for? Virtue used to be its own reward, but today Americans want a little something extra.

Part Three delves into raving, a word I use for deliberately throwing off self-control. Barney asks viewers to surrender to the outré beauty of the self-delight of his films. Whether he is videotaping himself crawling nude across an art gallery ceiling in Manhattan or bungee-jumping nude off Budapest's Chain Bridge, Barney delivers more than an adrenaline rush. The intellectual sparkle and strange glamour of his Cremaster Cycle stands as an allegory for the creative process itself, challenging received ideas about what is bad for us. Barney raves; he raises to an art form the naughtiness with which so many of us experiment in our private lives. His insights come to light at the limits of coherence, restraint, and beliefs about what's good for us. Beyond that, it bears mentioning that nudity never frightens Barney, although it continues to disarm many Americans. Whether in the snow-covered courtyards of Princeton University, at the Miss America Pageant, on Wall Street, or in the locker rooms of the University of Virginia, nudity will nudge its way onto center stage again and again in this book.

Part Three points out that we can rave together and regularly do. The wild party may not ultimately hurt anyone, but reveling in weakness might. Complex social pressures in modern America compel various groups to cling to ideas about themselves that do more harm than good, and raving fuels the doomed effort to force the world into our willfully mistaken vision of it.

The chief insight we must not lose sight of is that we are all too often our own worst enemies. Not infrequently, the suffering we bring on ourselves hurts more than the suffering the world foists upon us. There's physical pain and there's mental anguish. To be hit by a car has got to be very painful, but to hit someone else by accident and kill them has to be mentally excruciating—for most people, at least. When we get hit by a car through no fault of our own, the injuries we sustain are easier to bear by virtue of our innocence. We can blame our suffering on someone else. When we fall asleep at the wheel, however, or fail to pay attention or maybe drink and drive, any subsequent accident leaves us doubly stricken: We suffer because we are injured and we suffer because we lack another person to blame. Carnal escapades may involve another person, but we will come down awfully hard on ourselves later, when faced with a sexually transmitted disease or an unwanted pregnancy. We will likely face the trouble alone, blaming ourselves for having dropped our guard.

The realization that our problems are our own fault stings. Not surprisingly, it is a legal truism that the most dangerous witness to a defense case is the defendant him or herself, as the defendant rarely makes a fitting impression on judge or jury. This is what people mean when they say things like, "He's driving nails into his own coffin" or "Give him enough rope, and he'll hang himself." Very few of us will ever win a Darwin Award, but we will make stupid decisions in our own way.

This book, an invitation to study ourselves, raises more questions than it answers. Even just raising the questions, though, can help us understand how we engineer our own downfall, why dizzying reversals of fortune sometimes leave a trail leading back to those who should know better. Almost all of us have something to lose, and so we can take a lesson from those before us who fell back to earth. As we'll see, the lesson involves two kinds of loss: of self-control and of our very self. The second kind involves rocketing out of a shell into a new identity; it is more interesting than the first. But we won't be able to understand the second kind without discussing the first. For when we leap to a new identity, we appear to others to be "losing it."

Various religious and social institutions work to prevent us from losing self-control. Ironically, what we call self-control comes down to accepting someone else's control over us. And so it is questionable whether we'll be able to create new selves without shaking off self-control. In any event, many of us ultimately prefer feeling guilty to feeling powerless, and so we leap.

part one

Bad for Us

chapter one

Bad for Us

TIMES CHANGE, WE ALL KNOW. WHAT EXACTLY DOES TIME change, though? And what difference does it make to us?

Shifts in the general culture alter what we see in the mirror and subtly dictate what we wear, where we live, how we vote, and when we decide to lower our expectations of life. Looking back on Hollywood films that scandalized American moralists in the 1950s and 1960s (such as *Tea and Sympathy, Peyton Place, A Streetcar Named Desire, Cat on a Hot Tin Roof,* or *Midnight Cowboy*), it can be hard to understand what all the fuss was about. How could the mere whiff of illicit sexuality (as opposed to a graphic depiction of it) have titillated anyone? The answer must involve our expectations: We have an idea of moral fault lines we can't see, and we thrill to the thought we have crossed over one.

Our neighbors can penalize us for harming them; we can end up in jail, for example. Well over two thousand years ago, Socrates found himself on death row, blamed for corrupting the morals of Athens's next generation. Around the time of the Inquisition, Roman Catholic moralists made a point of indexing forbidden books, even burning them in town squares. Early in the twentieth century, many Germans believed that with the Jews, something impure had penetrated German music and painting. Jewish and so-called dissident artists found their "degenerate art" condemned, removed from public access.[1]

We proceed at our own risk, even through a world that seems friendly enough. How quickly things can change.

1

Well in the 1960s, it was against the law for white people to marry black people in several American states. Social rebels who defied the law ended up in jail. No one was supposed to fall in love with someone of a different skin color. Now, however, multi-racial couples pass us everywhere—at the mall, on the beach, around us at church. How did we get here?

School desegregation disrupted many American communities in the 1950s and 1960s. Photographs of standoffs at various public schools record a change then deemed bad for society. Today, arguments over vouchers in American schools continue to reflect the worries of an earlier day. Today, however, class substitutes for race as the bugbear in America. It is perhaps only a coincidence that people of color predominate the lower class.

Television shows, no less than jazz music and "rock and roll," had a lot to do with evolving attitudes about race. In the 1970s, Americans could watch *The Jeffersons*, a sitcom that included a happily married black-white couple. That popular show sparked new discussions of interracial dating and marriage. A Coca-Cola advertisement from January 1979 seemed to ignite a wave of fellow-feeling between blacks and whites.[2] When "Mean Joe" Greene of the Pittsburgh Steelers accepted a Coke from an adoring white boy, racial tension seemed to ease further. Other advertisers mimed the format of this television spot and featured similar glimpses of blacks and whites enjoying each other's company.

Television helped transform gender expectations as well. *The Mary Tyler Moore Show* dominated media rankings throughout the 1970s. In various interviews, Mary Tyler Moore has described the anxiety television networks felt about the basic story line of her show. A single woman who has recently broken up with her live-in boyfriend, Mary Richards is determined to make a success of her job and to live on her own. In the early 1970s, television executives worried over taking so bold a step as this. After all, who would watch over Mary and protect her from the sexual advances of men? (Only a decade earlier, Moore had starred in the *Dick Van Dyke* show, the producers of which insisted on portraying a married couple as sleeping in separate beds.) Some viewers might even suspect Mary was actually a prostitute of sorts, it was feared. Instead, America embraced the nonvirgin career girl Mary Richards and rooted for her success in the competitive world of broadcast news.

Conflicts jump from other social suspicions. Prior to the election of John F. Kennedy, for example, Roman Catholic presidential candidates faced an uphill battle in the United States. Americans worried that a Catholic president would dutifully hand his country over to the pope in Rome. Kennedy laid to rest some of this fear.

Scores of other examples of social change might round out the point that decisions we internalize as risky (such as taking an apartment of our own or dating someone of another race) depend on what the larger culture believes. After his election, John F. Kennedy could count on the media protecting him: They would not mention his adulterous affairs to the American public. But nearly forty years later, the American media bombarded the world with reports of President Bill Clinton's dalliance with a White House intern, Monica Lewinsky. In the 1990s, the American public largely forgave their adulterous president, remarkably. Something had changed: Even as Americans got more serious about sexual harassment (which became criminalized in the 1980s) and date rape, they got more lenient on sexual adventurers. Kennedy and Clinton both got lucky, each in his own way.

Or to take a far more pressing example: Throughout most of the twentieth century, the American media protected the police force. Random stories of mafia bribes or police brutality, such as the Rodney King incident that sparked riots in Los Angeles in the early 1990s, surfaced as puzzling aberrancies. Stories of racial profiling, in which white police officers stopped black motorists at disproportionately high rates, weakened public confidence in the integrity of police. At the very end of the twentieth century, a specific incident intensified the assault on the reputation of the police. New York Police Department Officer Justin Volpe beat Haitian immigrant Abner Louima, then sodomized him with a broomstick, then held the broomstick to his face. Officer Volpe had assumed that the traditional code of silence would protect him. He was wrong. He was forced to plead guilty in sniveling humiliation and was then sentenced to thirty years in prison. The media will no longer automatically protect politicians or policemen, and so politicians and policemen can do grave harm to themselves by assuming they can get away with anything.

So it is faceless others who collectively fight over and subtly dictate what's bad for us. Who cares anymore about learning that an aspiring politician once slept with someone of his own sex, or someone not his wife? We can't extort money from the homosexual or the philanderer, or at least not so easily. If the art of sexual blackmail has died, our rivals and enemies will have to find a new Achilles heel.

Blowing the whistle on rule-breakers gets harder as rules disappear. Not so long ago in the United States and the United Kingdom, divorce used to cut you off from polite society. English novels of social manners regularly featured divorced people who had to move to the Continent to escape the disapproval of fellow Brits (think of Mrs. Wallace Simpson and the king she seduced). Divorce presented an enormous challenge to the political ambitions of Adlai Stevenson and, several decades later, Nelson Rockefeller. In England, Princess Margaret dutifully decided against marrying the divorced man she loved and then spent the rest of her life regretting it as various members of the Royal Family themselves divorced. By the time the 1980 presidential candidate Ronald Reagan bothered to defend his prior divorce, the issue had largely died.

It used to be the kiss of death for Hollywood actors to find themselves outed as homosexuals. Even if the public thought you might be gay, they would transfer their loyalty or enthusiasm to another actor. On September 19, 1997, the *New York*

Times reported that heterosexual actors need no longer fear accepting homosexual roles.[3] Reasons cited for the change in climate included fresher scripts that made homosexuals less stereotypical and the transformative effect of the AIDS crisis, which may have focused attention on gay people in sympathetic ways. In the autumn of 2002, the *New York Times* and the *Boston Globe* began publishing same-sex wedding announcements. And then in June 2003, the United States Supreme Court ruled in *Lawrence v. Texas* that members of the same gender may enjoy sexual intimacy, free from state interference, in the privacy of their own home. (That decision overturned the 1986 ruling of *Bowers v. Hardwick*.)

Medical treatment to "cure" homosexuals has largely drifted into the past. Documentaries such as *Changing Our Minds* that depict the electroshock therapy used to transform the sexuality of gays and lesbians well into the 1960s strike contemporary college students as torture.[4] Heterosexuals found liberation in the 1960s as well; birth control has perhaps changed popular sensibility more than any other twentieth-century medical advance.

The list of cultural shifts conjures up nostalgic images of yesterday. Whether it's women in pants, the class system, plastic surgery, or being an unmarried mother, times have changed. Those changes affect not only politicians and movie stars, but ordinary citizens as well. Botox has made wrinkles a thing of the past, and ordinary women have begun to complain about the pressure they feel to undergo near monthly injections of the neurotoxin (derived from the bacteria *Clostridia botulinum*, the cause of botulism). Similar pressures thwart the unmarried or uncoupled; now that the stigma previously attached to adult on-line dating has apparently faded, you need a pretty good excuse to forego the new technology and its promise of coupledom.[5]

Harming others differs from harming ourselves, but prevailing social attitudes provide the interpretive lens for both. Our neighbors can still penalize us for harming ourselves: Although they may not be able to get us imprisoned, they can raise suspicion about our sanity, or the strength of our character. Manners and morals blur here, but we are rarely free from the scrutiny of others. While contemporary Americans enjoy more personal freedom than ever before, they do not exactly rule supreme over their private lives. In this age of unprecedented civil liberties, any remaining no-nos assume even greater curiosity. We chart our personal trajectories by these no-nos.

Assumptions about who our friends are often stem from cultural currents. These currents shift, sometimes with dramatic speed. Keeping our finger on the pulse of our world pays off in unexpected ways. Knowing what others think is bad for us is what our parents and friends hope we'll learn. When we defy the majority, they lie in wait to use our misfortunes against us. "That's just what you had coming to you," we may hear.

Thrown back upon ourselves, pondering from our punishment how we got into this mess, we can hardly ignore the inevitable questions weighing down on us: Who am I? What do I want, and what can I do?

chapter two

Are We Not Our Own?

AN ANCIENT GREEK PHILOSOPHER'S EXHORTATION BROKERS many of our decisions: Become who you are! We moderns yearn for self-actualization, as the talk show hosts put it. The majestic self, the priceless core in every human, basks in the glory we lavish upon it. From different corners we hear its praises—from the Oracle at Delphi, which counseled us "Know thyself," to Socrates, who warned us that the unexamined life is not worth living, to a barrage of popular magazines. Consequently, the root of most personal problems—at least in the first world—must be the self, which occasionally stumbles or loses its way. Satisfaction with life, our very happiness, hinges on understanding what it means to harm, abandon, or betray ourselves.

Toward the end of his *Confessions,* a book to which many television talk shows indirectly owe their inspiration, Augustine writes, "I have become a problem to myself."[1] What could that mean? What exactly is a self? A working description surfaces in William James's *Principles of Psychology* (1890; 1:291):

> *In its widest possible sense . . . a man's Self is the sum total of all that he CAN call his,* not only his body and his psychic powers, but his clothes and his house, his wife and children, his ancestors and friends, his reputation and works, his lands and horses, and yacht and bank-account. . . . If they wax and prosper, he feels triumphant: if they dwindle and die away, he feels cast down—not necessarily in the same degree for each thing, but in much the same way for all. [emphasis in original]

Notice that James includes friends and belongings in the self's domain, instead of excising them, as ascetics do. Regardless of how far we draw the self's boundaries from our bodies, becoming who we are requires self-control. Without self-control, we risk becoming sybarites, angry monsters, couch potatoes, or crybabies. At least in the abstract, princesses, nuns, spies, and movie stars personify self-control. It's not a vigorous asceticism they display but a natural restraint. They govern themselves prudently and sometimes intimidate us with a frosty firmness.

The word self-control can mean not only this awesome command but also autonomy, the idea that we can decide for ourselves who to be and what to do. More so than ever before in Western democracies, individuals can express themselves autonomously. They dress as they like, make love as they see fit, and decide for themselves where to work. To many people, kings, queens, and even religious authorities appear relics of the past. We have made ourselves kings and queens instead. We control ourselves.

Or do we? Certainly modern democracies prohibit us from harming others. How and why do those democracies prohibit or strongly discourage us from doing to ourselves whatever we care to? Why, for example, can we not sell ourselves into slavery, smoke marijuana in our homes, drive without a seat belt, or auction off one of our kidneys? Why do others frown when we use tobacco, ride a bicycle without a helmet, work on a suntan, reveal embarrassing secrets on a TV talk show, pose nude for the camera, have our tongue surgically split in two, refuse psychotherapy or resist medical attention, live beyond our financial means, roar at cars driving slowly in the fast lane, indulge in extreme sports, or suffer for beauty (as in face lifts, nose jobs, breast implants, and penile enlargement operations)? In the name of friendship, others may blame us for what they suppose are ways of hurting ourselves. They may pass judgment on the way we navigate the stress and strain of busy schedules or the extent to which we tolerate the soul-battering consequences of working for a living. They try to hold us accountable to them.

They also try to use us against ourselves. This is an intriguing strategy. In July 2001, for example, the Roman Catholic bishops of South Africa publicly and somewhat remarkably claimed that condoms cause AIDS rather than prevent it. According to the statement read by Cardinal Wilfred Napier: "Condoms may be one of the main reasons for the spread of HIV/AIDS. Apart from the possibility of condoms being faulty or wrongly used, they contribute to the breaking down of self-control and mutual trust." This tactic of playing the self-control trump card has long appealed to both religious groups and secular governments. If they can't quite put you in jail for masturbating or attempting suicide, if they can't consign you to a mental asylum for a gambling habit or reliance on public welfare, they can always accuse you of a self-control problem.

Caring for the Elusive Self

"To be oneself," you say, is all-important. But is one's self really worth the effort? — PAUL VALÉRY

The easiest question in the world—"Who am I?"—ends up plaguing many of us. See for yourself how hard it can be to moor your past into your present, and you will likely agree. Pinning down your innermost core, deciding whether you even believe it's there, takes a lot of work. Once you manage that, you can then turn to other tricky questions, such as what you owe yourself, and others.

To the extent that we prize the self, we naturally nurture it. Given how quickly it may slip away from us, we may find ourselves clinging to any trace of it that seems to flatter us. We may also find ourselves cringing at the thought of compromising our selves. Even a single night of drunken revelry can scare us: Who knows what we might do? So can love, which may throw us perilously off balance and undermine clarity about who we are. In *Wuthering Heights,* passion erupts between two of the more famous lovers in British literature, Cathy and Heathcliff. Cathy is soon parted from Heathcliff, the real love of her life, though a social outcast, and she declares: "I *am* Heathcliff." Though she marries well, she cannot put aside her romantic view of life; only the next generation will reconcile passion with social order.

Aging also pries us away from ourselves, or the image of ourselves that anchors our past. This intuition no doubt plays into the American obsession to hold on to youth. Although it would be just as easy to argue that we become more fully, more authentically ourselves as we age, many hold on to youth as the touchstone of who they really are. In Gore Vidal's novel *Hollywood,* the thoughts of an older man race along the body of a much younger companion, who yields himself physically. Blaise, the older man, encounters his distant self in the torso of someone else:

> In recent years, Blaise had indulged so little in masculine pleasures that he had almost forgotten just how splendid it was to be with a body that was the same as his but entirely different, and young. More than anything, the other's youth acted as a trigger to both lust and memory, and Blaise was, suddenly, *briefly,* as one with his original self.[2]

Aging amounts to a fall of sorts, at least in a culture as body-conscious as the Hollywood of which Vidal writes. How sadly Adam and Eve must have reminisced about the Garden of Eden; how wistfully the elderly or physically incapacitated must ponder youthful health. Aging disrupts our identity and compels us to adjust our notion of where we fit into the social pecking order. Listen to how American writer James Carroll makes sense of a Catholic boyhood long gone by, while pondering an old photo of himself:

By now, the effort to recall this phase of my personal history has succeeded at least in evoking my sad pity for the affected, frightened lad in this photograph with the freckles, big ears, and mini-pompadour; his carefully constructed surface—that Windsor knot just so—layering over a seething insecurity; his dread of a future that seemed a trap or a dead end; the tumult of his hidden unbelief, sex, and filial subservience. This lad whose brothers knew nothing about him, and whose parents could see only in the unsteady light of choices they themselves had made twenty-five years before. This lad whose ability to be consoled by a sweet, pretty girl who claimed to love him, who'd trusted him with her near nakedness, was blown to smithereens by the certain knowledge that, despite himself, in every gesture of affection and word of promise he had lied to her about an open future. This lad—in seeing him in this photo now, I would love to embrace him, pressing in all that I have seen and learned of acceptance and forgiveness and affirmation. He is my younger self, of course, and there is nothing I can do for him.[3]

While we may insist that our past is our own, we may feel eerily disconnected from it (victims of physical or psychological abuse, unfortunately, will often feel imprisoned by their past). James Carroll feels about the picture of the young boy he had been the way devoted parents feel about a headstrong child: ultimately helpless to prevent the inevitable. The endless fracturing and gluing, cutting and pasting that go into hammering the self can make us feel oddly artificial, arbitrary.

Self-identity lies at the heart of caring for the self: In order to nurture a self beyond providing for its material needs, you have to know something about that self. Then you have to balance a duty to discover and cultivate the self against an obligation to care for others. Western thinking has privileged duties to others over duties to the self. Christianity in particular has maligned love of self as a human defect, a fall from grace, a manifestation of pride (the worst of the seven deadly sins).

Self-love must be sinful and therefore not really love at all. The modern world, despite its robust enthusiasm for selfhood, still bears vestiges of a disapproving past. We must love ourselves, then, but not too much. The point of taking care of ourselves, on a conservative view, would be to grow into the best possible source of support to others. We would care for ourselves to benefit others, not ourselves.

It took many centuries for a proper, sustained focus on the self to surface. Norbert Elias traced the course of this focus in *The Civilizing Process*. Writing in 1939, he took up the subject of public nose-picking:

> And, as with other childish habits, the medical warning [against picking one's nose] now appears alongside or in place of the social one as an instrument of conditioning, in the reference to the injury that can be done by doing "such a thing" too often.... Up to this time [the end of the eighteenth century], habits are almost always judged expressly in their relation to other people, and they are forbidden at least in the secular upper class, because they may be troublesome or embarrassing to others, or because they betray a "lack of respect." Now habits are condemned more and more as such, not in regard to others. In this way, socially undesirable impulses or inclinations are more radically repressed. They are associated with embarrassment, fear, shame, or guilt, even when one is alone. Much of what we call "morality" or "moral" reasons has the same function as "hygiene" or "hygienic" reasons: to condition children to a certain social standard. Molding by such means aims at making socially desirable behavior automatic, a matter of self-control, causing it to appear in the consciousness of the individual as the result of his own free will, and in the interests of his own health or human dignity.[4]

As the middle class came to internalize these mores, he goes on to say, conflict between socially inadmissible impulses or tendencies and the pattern of social demands anchored in the individual took on the sharply defined form central to modern psychological theories—above all, to psychoanalysis. Physical and moral health are things we owe to others, Elias saw. We must remain in good health in order to make life easier for our neighbors. Duties to the self are as much social as personal; this is the same logic to which the South African Roman Catholic bishops appealed when they claimed that condoms cause HIV/AIDS.

Judaism and Christianity have had a good deal to say about duties to the self, which are grounded in duties to God. The first four commandments concern what we owe God and the last six, how we should treat other people. The commandments exhort us to fulfill a duty to ourselves to be moral. This duty occasionally takes very specific forms. Reading Leviticus today, for example, we learn that we must swear off tattooing and the wearing of cotton-polyester blends. In the New Testament, St. Paul instructs that we are not our own, but rather God's. If our lands and very bodies are on loan from God, it follows that He will expect us to care properly for His gifts. Thus, for example, something potentially as solitary as masturbation is forbidden because it disappoints God by abusing the genitals, which were not intended for such use. Proper sexual conduct is part of the proper care of the self. Both Hebrew and Christian scriptures pit the self against God.

Contemporary moral culture in the West reveals the influence of Leviticus and St. Paul. Here is how one gay man remembers the physical examination he had to undergo in Detroit in 1969, prior to service in the Vietnam War. The attending physician listened to another would-be soldier admit his homosexuality and castigated him:

> "Your body is God's temple. How dare you defile it with perversion!" the doctor spat out loud enough for everyone to hear. Most of us got only ten or fifteen seconds at his station before we were passed on, but this boy had to stand, shivering, humiliated, for ten minutes as the doctor ranted on about "vile sickness."[5]

Women who have abortions harbor similar stories of Right-to-lifers posted outside medical clinics and hurling abuse at them. When other people insist that we take what they perceive to be proper care of ourselves, they may invoke God (even when they hold secular positions) in order to drive home their revulsion and level of interest in our affairs.

It may be that a shift to the kind of officious meddling in others' lives reflected in the passage above is a shift that signifies the desired end as a matter of entitlement, not spiritual grace. That shift is interesting. The moral person hopes for proof that other people feel a duty to him, but treats the appearance of such evidence as a wondrous thing (Schopenhauer, for example, considered human kindness the great mystery of ethics).

An economic dimension further encases the question of harm to the self. Nowadays, for example, we may oppose smoking because of implicit costs to ourselves, via a national health care system. People who end up on public support cost us something. If they do not take care of themselves, we will have to pay—literally. Consider the following transcript from a penalty hearing held before Santa Clara superior court judge Gerald Chargin in September 1969. On the advice of his lawyer, the seventeen-year-old defendant, a Mexican-American boy, had pled guilty to the charge of incest with his fifteen-year-old sister. Both the lawyer and the boy wanted to avoid a trial, to which an innocent plea would undoubtedly lead. This is what the judge said to a boy (who may well have been innocent):

THE COURT: Don't you know that things like this are terribly wrong? This is one of the worst crimes that a person can commit. I just get so disgusted that I just figure what is the use? You are just an animal. You are lower than an animal Even animals don't do that. You are pretty low.

I don't know why your parents haven't been able to teach you anything or train you. Mexican people, after 13 years of age, it's perfectly all right to go out and act like an animal. It's not even right to do that to a stranger, let alone a member of your own family. I don't have much hope for you. You will probably end up in State's Prison before you are 25, and that's where you belong, any how. There is nothing much you can do.

I think you haven't got any moral principles. You won't acquire anything. Your parents won't teach you what is right or wrong and won't watch out.

Apparently your sister is pregnant; is that right?

THE MINOR'S FATHER, MR. CASILLAS: Yes.

THE COURT: It's a fine situation. How old is she?

THE MINOR'S MOTHER, MRS. CASILLAS: Fifteen.

THE COURT: Well, probably she will have half a dozen children and three or four marriages before she is 18.

The County will have to take care of you. You are no particular good to anybody. We ought to send you out of the country—send you back to Mexico. You belong in prison for the rest of your life for doing things of this kind. You ought to commit suicide. That's what I think of people of this kind. You are lower than animals and haven't the right to live in organized society— just miserable, lousy, rotten people.[6]

Racial bigotry combines with fiscal concern (and perhaps a certain sexual fascination) to produce this unusual articulation of cruelty. The judge explicitly reduces the Mexican-American boy to animal status and upbraids him for soaking up public resources. The responsible have to pay for the mistakes of the irresponsible, this judge laments. Religious people have long viewed self-control as a remedy for sin; non-religious people can just as easily appeal to self-control as the supreme weapon against crime and tax increases.

It is easy to decry the selfishness and hard heart of this superior court judge. And yet American reluctance to pay for other people's mistakes sits well with Teddy Roosevelt's rugged individualism and Ronald Reagan's economic policies. The moral dimensions of such questions undergird political skirmishes. We owe good behavior not just to ourselves, but to our community, which cannot run smoothly without our cooperation. For, as Yogi Berra once quipped, there are no rules if everyone's breaking 'em.

The whole notion of being true to ourselves, like the category "Bad for Us," relies on the gold standard of the authentic self. After years of psychotherapy or watching television talk shows, we may still fidget over the question of how we'll know when we've discovered our authentic self. We'll just know it, we are assured by the guides we find for sale around us.

Belief in God above reinforces belief in the soul within, which many believers have considered synonymous with the "authentic self" that lies at the heart of so many self-help books. How will those who have given up on God above maintain belief in the gold standard within, this "authentic self"? Will they choose to believe still that the self is discovered, or will they opt instead to think of *inventing* that reality? The jury is still out.

We Westerners have inherited a tradition of believing that we *discover* our true self. Even as belief in God has declined in importance, the way it has conditioned us to think about identity has remained. We'll see that philosophers and politicians have justified interfering with our freedom to do what we want with ourselves by arguing that what we do to ourselves infringes on a superior right of someone else. And so we are not our own. We answer to our neighbors, political leaders, and perhaps God as well.

Kant, the Killjoy

Who says we have duties to ourselves? And what are those duties?

Immanuel Kant (d. 1804) towers over other thinkers and stands as the single most influential philosopher of the last three centuries. In his *Lectures on Ethics* and *Metaphysics of Morals* he devotes several sections to the fundamental question of why can't we do to ourselves whatever we please. What is the moral basis of any duty to the self? Kant tells us that although we cannot be autonomous or even authentically human without freedom, all wickedness comes from freedom. Thus freedom is both good and bad.

Take the freedom to end it all, for example. Kant forbids suicide. The duty to remain among the living until death takes us naturally has to do with something much bigger than ourselves, namely humanity. Disposing of oneself as a mere means to some discretionary end debases humanity, Kant explains. Humanity is the reason why we can't do lots of other things to or with ourselves. The duty to resist lust or carnal self-degradation, for instance, follows from the fact that they violate humanity in one's own person and the duty to avoid drunkenness, from the fact that the drunkard is "like a mere animal," and cannot be "treated as a human being." Lying "violates the dignity of humanity in one's own person"; and the self-respect opposed to servility is a duty "with reference to the dignity of humanity within us."

With the exception of lying, these duties concern our bodies. The human being's duty to develop its natural perfection is one "he owes himself (as a rational being)" because it is again "bound up with the end of humanity in our own person." Violation of the duty of gratitude, for example, is yet again "a rejection of one's own humanity in one's own person," while the duty to sympathize with others holds insofar as "the human being is regarded not merely as a rational being but as an animal endowed with reason." All three duties of respect to others (those against self-love, contempt, and giving scandal) are grounded on the dignity in other human beings. Kant locates the duty to promote our own moral perfection in the same motivation that prompts us to want to be good people. That motivation is explicitly grounded in our dignity as rational beings: Our duty to avoid avarice is defended on the ground that it impairs our rational nature in respect of the use of money (self-impairment is also the basis for the proscription of drunkenness).[7]

For Kant, what's bad for us basically comes down to anything that violates our dignity. The most influential philosophical account of dignity can be found in Kant's *Groundwork of the Metaphysics of Morals*.[8] Kant resolves the conflict between dignity and personal autonomy through a technical distinction between the noumenal and phenomenal self. In the first realm, the demands of dignity affect everyone identically; in the second realm, life in the real world prompts certain "inclinations" which lure us off the moral path. When we lose our way, disregarding our moral compass, we betray ourselves. This is how Kant solves the apparent restriction on freedom of choice.

Each individual is a link in the chain of humanity. Keeping the chain strong deserves our full, collective support. Whether children share the same duties to the self as adults is very hard to say. Try as we may to instruct children about their moral duty, their imagination may take them to a never-never land of beanstalks, glass slippers, and mothers living in shoes. We ourselves encourage children to play; their games may contrast sharply with our regimen of reason and regulation. Should children's play go too far, it may lead to strict punishment from embarrassed or irritated adults. John Stuart Mill (d. 1873) thought that we should deny liberty to children and savages because they don't have the capacity to conceive of and follow through on long-range plans. They may be able to obey, but they cannot exercise self-control. A developed person can be left to make his or her own mistakes, because developed people possess the capacities for learning from mistakes.

If the self is really as important as the ancient Greeks and contemporary self-help gurus insist, then it makes sense to empower the government, our religious leaders, and even our neighbors to force us to honor our duty to ourself. For we both lose and win when we violate a duty to the self. If we consciously decide not to pursue a talent for singing, we lose a potentially brilliant career but gain the freedom that comes with having made up our own mind. And if we have a duty to develop our talents, can we ever be called selfish? Doesn't thinking principally of ourself all the time amount to a moral way of life? Not exactly, as we'll see.

No, and Why Not

Kant's idea of the good life may not strike us as particularly compelling today, yet it has done more to shape American morals than any other influence, save the Bible. Let's bear down on the question of self-harm, what we're not supposed to do to ourselves. Perhaps copying the format of the Ten Commandments, Kant condemned the following classes of persons in the *Lectures on Ethics:*

1. drunkard
2. ingratiator ("boot licker")
3. class clown, or town fool ("camping it up")
4. liar
5. freeloader
6. whiner
7. laborer
8. whipping-boy
9. suicide (almost the worst thing you can do to yourself)
10. homosexual (abhorrent—the very thought of it induces vomiting)

Two hundred years later, the list will still find supporters. Kant explains that anyone who fits into a category listed above "degrades his person and loses his manhood."[9] Anticipating the modern-day terminology of "victimless crimes," Kant concludes that those who harm themselves harm all of humanity, for they fail to uphold the intrinsic dignity of being human. "We must reverence humanity in our own person," Kant insists time and again. Each of us serves as an ambassador of sorts for the human race, and our every move should indicate the respect due such marvelous creatures.

Kant will strike many modern readers as anachronistic, as he seems to think of all people as heterosexual. For one bad reason or another (for example, lack of a suitable partner of the opposite gender, curiosity, or willful perversity), some men (and Kant means men) choose to have sex with other men. Today, most well-educated Westerners believe that a small percentage of humans are intrinsically and permanently attracted to members of their own sex. A man making love to another man isn't necessarily losing control of himself; he may simply be following his natural urges.

Kant's fear of what man could become if he dropped his guard would seem to confirm that we are our own enemies. Inside us lurks a destructive power that can bring us down, quite apart from the ill will our competitors may feel toward us. We have to keep an eye on ourselves if we wish to be moral. He who gives free rein to his inclinations, according to Kant, sinks lower than an animal. Animals, after all, have no choice in the matter:

> But if a man gives free rein to his inclinations, he sinks lower than an animal because he then lives in a state of disorder which does not exist among animals. A man is then in contradiction with the essential ends of humanity in his own person, and so with himself.[10]

And so we find ourselves back at self-control. It should be clear by now that self-control prevents us from sliding somewhere we don't want to go.

Another reason we should not do whatever we like to ourselves comes from natural law theory. Although the most famous natural law enthusiast of all time must remain St. Thomas Aquinas, ancient Greek and Roman philosophers had earlier appealed to eternal laws of nature to justify their theories. Following Aquinas, Christian philosophers strove to prove that the principles of morality could be worked out by reason alone (much as Kant would do later). Even without the benefit of holy scriptures then (that is, the New Testament) all the peoples of the world would be able to discern independently the proper way to live. Only people were bound by the natural law, because only people possessed the reason with which to apprehend the moral law.

Some contemporary philosophers, although few in number, still appeal to the natural law as an entree into God's eternal reason. Arguing that homosexuality, like abortion, is intrinsically evil, Princeton professor Robert George contends:

> To the extent that the law embodies a legislative concern to prevent individuals from demeaning, degrading, or destroying themselves, it treats [every individual's] welfare as just as important as everyone else's. In seeking to uphold public morals, it favors the moral well-being of each and every member of the public. No one's interest in living a worthy and dignified life is singled out as more or less important.[11]

The natural law requires supplementing by human laws. Although human laws can vary from community to community, they must always respect the limits of the law of nature in order to obligate people. God engraved the most basic principles of the natural law in the minds of all (which is not to say that everyone is equally capable of understanding the complexity of natural law).

The natural law approach clashes with both the liberal and libertarian view of homosexuality. The examples I have considered, taken together, should not be interpreted as an argument in favor of libertarianism, a political philosophy assigning primacy to individual rights, but rather a philosophical question about why our culture is the way it is.

Libertarians believe that each person has the right to live his or her life in any way he or she chooses, so long as he respects the equal rights of others. Provided that our individual actions don't infringe on others, libertarians oppose government restrictions on individual behavior. That doesn't necessarily mean approving or endorsing any particular behavior; it just means that the coercive power of the state should be limited to protecting our rights. We tend to identify particular civil liberties as the state attempts to restrict them and it would be impossible to list all the civil liberties presently available to us. The Bill of Rights reflected the Founders' specific experience with British restrictions on individual rights; but, recognizing that it was impossible to enumerate all individual rights, they added the Ninth Amendment—reserving to individuals other rights not enumerated—and the Tenth Amendment—reiterating that the federal government has only those powers set out in the Constitution.[12]

Civil libertarians may find themselves defending an individual's right to engage in something they find reprehensible. Freedom will usher in some unpleasantness, just as Kant warned. We all benefit from the general condition of freedom, not just because it entitles us to do what we want, but because civilization progresses through trial and error, through individuals' trying new ways of life. Civil libertarians maintain that the freedom that will be used by only one man or woman in a million may be more important to society and more beneficial to the majority than any freedom that we all use.

Libertarians defend the right of individuals to freedom of speech, freedom of the press, and freedom of broadcast, even though they may exercise that freedom in ways that offend others in society, whether through sexually explicit language, racist magazines, or burning flags. Libertarians celebrate the difficulty of censoring and regulating the fabulously complex Internet, for governments will be increasingly hard-pressed to limit what their citizens can know.

In the name of protecting our safety, government restricts the right to make our own decisions and assume responsibility for the consequences of those decisions. Mandatory seatbelt and helmet laws, for instance, deny us the right to choose the risks we are willing to assume. The Food and Drug Administration denies us the right to choose the vitamins, pharmaceutical drugs, and medical devices we want (think of Laetril here in the 1970s, the early anti-AIDS experimental drugs in the 1980s, and the "home abortion" drug RU-40 of the 1990s). Libertarians insist that the decision to pursue a particular course of medication is as personal and intimate as any choice could be.

Although I do not want to advocate libertarianism (or any political agenda) here, I do note the coincidence of the questions I raise and the positions for which libertarians have fought. Kant was no libertarian. His philosophy culminated in the attempt to provide a purely moral foundation for traditional theological claims. And so whether you believe in God or not, you had to agree that the theologians were right about moral conduct, or so Kant thought. He strove to demonstrate that pure rational thought had an absolute claim on all of us.

According to Kant, we have no right to harm ourselves.

Who We Hope to Be

Kant deserves credit for articulating the moral (as opposed to theological) basis of duties to the self, which is making ourselves worthy of the human name. The good of fulfilling these duties, further, is that we become better company for others when we strengthen ourselves. Through fulfillment of the self, we weave ourselves to our neighbors. They see themselves in us, and we in them. The point of working on ourselves, we hear, is to help others. But we are left with conflicting arguments, for we can just as easily conceive of virtue as something we achieve in private, sequestered from the world. The difference, we'll see, matters as much to rule-following as to rule-breaking.

Generation after generation, Kant's warnings have seeped into the awareness of many Westerners and shaped the delicate sense of how we rate as a person. Kant's warnings have added to the emotional wreckage wrought by the thoughtless pursuit of instant gratification. As we lead our private lives amidst others, the list of duties to the self has expanded to include watching our weight, cutting down on television time, monitoring our relationship to the (potentially addicting) Internet, watching our cholesterol levels, saving for retirement, and managing stress. These new duties reflect old ways of caring for the self.

In an era that has explicitly praised autonomy and directed us to "follow our bliss," customs and laws of different sorts inhibit us from doing so. As the opportunities for selves to expand and blossom have increased over time, the restrictions on what we can do to ourselves have not diminished much. This is as true for the bohemians of the world as it is for the bourgeoisie. And this helps explain why a walk on the wild side, stepping out of bounds, retains its delicious kick.

chapter three

Flights of Fancy: A Tour

"I adore recklessness." —SUSAN SONTAG, *In America*

THE FOLLOWING TOUR OF WHAT WE ARE NOT ALLOWED to do with ourselves might seem to lack philosophical seriousness, might even seem the moral equivalent of the Travel Channel. But tourism of this kind may amount to the best way of teaching ethics.

Kant has explained how exactly we harm ourselves. Our happiness, our success in life, is supposedly what's at stake when others object that something is bad for us. A panoramic view of self-harm would include examples as diverse as "economy-class syndrome" (air travelers must beware the danger of blood clots causing pulmonary embolisms during long bouts of sitting in confined spaces) and the "death with dignity" controversy (asking a doctor to help you end your life in the face of terrible pain and a terminal diagnosis). I steer clear of the life-and-death issues here, along with Kant.

The very idea of hurting others by harming ourselves begs the question of the extent to which morality involves other people. Is morality intrinsically social? Think about a man stranded on a desert island for years: Is he capable of acting immorally? Certainly, if you allow belief in God, the answer is yes. But even if you don't, most people will agree that it would be immoral for him to commit suicide, to mutilate his body for entertainment, or to have sex with animals on the island. Early Christians meditated in the desert with great enthusiasm; they took their moral ideals with them and, in solitude, they lived austere lives. We, like they, take moral expectations with us when we travel.

Let's travel now. Let's tour the moral expectations that we probably first confronted as adolescents—and that our children will also likely encounter as they grow up. Let's think about the following specific examples of harm to the self: masturbation; selling ourselves into slavery; prostitution; humiliating ourselves on talk shows; stripping before the camera; failing to strive to reach our potential; drug abuse; and self-neglect. These examples would not be worth our time if it weren't for the fact that we might want or need to do them, at least on occasion.

The list could easily get weird and scary. We've all heard of bestiality, though we've probably never heard anyone indicate anything but revulsion to it. Few of us have heard of apotemnophilia, the condition used to describe people who want to be amputees. Hard as it is to believe, some people have enlisted a physician to amputate a limb for no medical reason. When doctors have refused to participate in these procedures, determined individuals have amputated themselves at home.[1] In a different yet related vein, the idea of poor people selling their organs in order to help their families has frightened Americans into criminalizing such transactions. Clearly, we may not do with our bodies whatever we like.

Even weirder and scarier is a pair of German men that found in 2001 they could satisfy one another beautifully. One had always fantasized about eating another person. The other had long fantasized about being eaten. We can only speculate about the sexual heights these two men reached together in a case that kept German and British newspapers buzzing for weeks. What makes the case profoundly disturbing is the fact that the deceased cooperated fully in the *pas de deux*. Jürgen Brandes allowed Armin Miewes to amputate his penis; the two ate it together after Miewes sauteed it with herbs. Then Miewes stabbed Brandes to death, videotaping the entire event.[2]

Miewes was only caught when he went back to the Internet, posting new ads indicating his hope to find another participant/victim. In the ensuing and highly publicized trial, Miewes admitted to the killing but insisted it wasn't murder, as he had done only what he had been asked to do.

Mine is a compromise list, one that largely steers away from pathologies, perversions, and heroism (of course, these notions are themselves open to dispute). Plato and Aristotle would have found this list baffling, ancient Jews and Christians would have found it bizarre, and residents of American ghettoes or barrios might find it unfair to them. Contemporary self-help magazines and self-improvement books largely stem from this list. Guilt and shame begin here, as does defiance. The list, not meant to be exhaustive, helps us peer out to the moral boundaries of our culture. At the same time, these prohibitions outline what it means to be properly human, or perhaps just a good American.

Masturbation and the Private Dancer

As a ready example of how we might harm ourselves in total isolation from other people, think of masturbation. Aside from the Roman Catholic hierarchy, virtually no one is troubled by masturbation anymore, yet Jocelyn Elders forfeited her job as Surgeon General of the United States in 1994 when she suggested that masturbation was an appropriate topic for classroom discussion. In 1994 it seemed reasonable to consider masturbation preferable to sexual contact, which could spread the deadly virus HIV/AIDS. Those Republican members of the House of Representatives who found masturbation morally repulsive called for her resignation (they had sparred with her over various other issues, but masturbation was the last straw). House Republicans won.

The subject had distressed many previous generations.[3] Masturbation is similar to—yet less public than—dancing:

both have been forbidden in different places and at different times over the centuries, but both have emerged in the contemporary world more or less vindicated.[4] Private dancing as a metaphor for masturbation would have struck our forebears as picaresque, yet the image seems strangely appropriate after reading condemnations of the respective sins. (Public dancing evoked even louder invective, although one finds no mention of public masturbation in medieval penitentials, self-help books, or moral guides.)

In masturbation we get an initial glimpse of how our forebears saw individuality and a sense of how the limits of morality have shifted.[5] Worried about the prevalence of masturbation among young French boys, a Dr. Demeaux issued an urgent call to the French Ministry of Culture in 1849. He demanded that teachers periodically surprise all school-age boys with body searches. According to Dr. Demeaux, masturbators would give themselves away by the large size of their manhood and by their fear of showing themselves naked.[6] So much for modesty.

Freud, who always disapproved of masturbation, blamed it and *coitus interruptus* for anxiety, lassitude, a plethora of hysterical symptoms—the emotional dysfunctions of his day. Toward the beginning of the twentieth century, some civic leaders accepted the responsibility of guarding young American men from themselves. "Dr. Luther Gulick, the preeminent leader of the YMCA's physical work, advocated frank discussion of sexuality with boys from an early age, combined with efforts to prevent masturbation and keep them away from pornography."[7]

Religious explanations differ from secular ones on the question of why masturbation should be avoided. Religious opposition sprang from the story of Onan (Genesis 38:7–10), who spilled his seed on the ground and brought on the fatal wrath of God. In the fifteenth century, St. Bernadino of Siena declared that (male) masturbation furnished more than adequate grounds for divorce.[8] Pope Pius XI wrote at the end of the nineteenth century, "The Divine Majesty regards with great detestation this horrible crime," by which he meant spilling one's seed upon the ground, or into a condom. Here is how Bernard Häring, likely the most influential Roman Catholic moral theologian of the twentieth century, articulates the standard Catholic opposition to the sin that carries the peculiar name of "self-abuse":

> This sin is also called pollution, masturbation, the solitary sin, and even onanism. The latter term, however, refers rather to selfish avoidance of conception in the sexual union. Self-abuse, or masturbation, is an unnatural deviation of the sexual craving to one's own sexual instinct and its complete satisfaction or gratification. This stands at variance with the urge in its natural finality which is directed to a partner of the other sex and seeks sexual satisfaction only in the orbit of such loving encounter. Wherefore the term *ipsation*, which means cramped and egotistic self-inclusion (the word derives from the Latin *ipse*), seems the most appropriate designation of the sin . . . [which] unmasks its hideous visage in moral morbidity, in corrosive influence, and in conflict with the natural orientation to marriage.[9]

Häring proceeds to explain that habitual self-abuse may take such a hold of an individual as to become an obsession or mania, wreaking havoc on health and especially on the nervous system. And what is worse than the deterioration of health, Häring writes, is the harmful effect on the character formation of the adolescent who yields to the vice without a struggle. Even though health may not be ruined unless the habit takes deep hold of the individual, the hazard is always present. Youth should be seriously warned of the danger. In this, Häring issues an old cry: For centuries, Catholic moralists had likened masturbation to blasphemy. That tradition largely follows Augustine, who considered masturbation morally worse than fornication. Even a man's having sex with his mother was preferable to masturbation, for wasting precious semen amounted to murder.

It is interesting that a Roman Catholic priest should talk about masturbation in the context of "a natural orientation to marriage." Since the Reformation a great many thinkers have gone on record as finding clerical celibacy, required by the Church of Rome, deeply worrying. Robert Burton (1577–1640), author of the enormously influential work *The Anatomy of Melancholy,* opposed the celibacy requirement of Catholic religious in part because, in his view, the solitary state encouraged masturbation.[10]

As I've said, the Catholic Church still considers masturbation a mortal sin, that is, lethal for the soul. In rare circumstances, masturbation can even be physically lethal. A 1981 *Hustler* article entitled "Orgasm of Death" brought to public attention the curious case of adventurers, most often male, who seek sexual excitement in cerebral hypoxia, that is to say diminishing the supply of oxygen to the brain during sexual stimulation. A nonpsychotic mental disorder, autoerotic asphyxia results from hanging, strangulation, chest compression, or covering the mouth and nose with a plastic bag or mask. Exerting pressure on the arteries of the neck constricts bloodflow to the brain and can apparently heighten sexual pleasure. People don't mean to kill themselves in autoerotic fatalities; the deaths occur accidentally, a result of miscalculated risk.[11]

Denise Danks's novel *The Pizza House Crash* uses this awful event as a plot device: A computer whiz in London jumps into detective mode when her cousin Julian dies from autoerotic asphyxiation.[12] In real life, the aftermath of this brand of self-abuse can bring further devastation than just death. In *Herceg v. Hustler Magazine Inc.,* a jury rejected the argument that the *Hustler* article had prompted a fourteen-year-old Texas boy to try it. The boy had mistakenly hanged himself while masturbating. The appellate ruling overturned a

$182,000 jury verdict against *Hustler* in a suit brought by the boy's mother and a friend. In 2002, American parents were still suing insurance companies that refused to reimburse them for the deaths of sons who had asphyxiated themselves while masturbating. Insurance companies argued that such deaths were not accidental, and American juries sided with them.[13]

Extreme examples aside, masturbation continues unabated. In July 2003, a team of Australian physicians concluded a study that seemed to link daily masturbation to a significant decrease in the likelihood of prostate cancer. Frequent ejaculation, they argued, cleanses the prostate gland and prevents cancer-causing agents from festering.[14]

Famous masturbators include Rousseau, Proust, English prime minister Gladstone, Ludwig Wittgenstein, and the American writers Thomas Wolfe and Philip Roth. Each of them was born long before the 1990s, when American television shows and Hollywood movies began to mainstream autoerotic adventures. Betty Dodson's popular book *Sex for One: The Joy of Selfloving* could hardly have even come to market two decades earlier, when old fears still prevailed.[15] We no longer worry that the people we rub elbows with might be masturbating at home. In the past, sharing company with someone suffering from "excessive and socially perverted nervous stimulation" could taint you. "The projection of anxieties about sexuality applied as well to domestic subjects of evangelization, as evidenced in YMCA missionary Charles Conrad Hamilton's extreme discomfort in socializing with lumbermen during his YMCA mission work in Wisconsin, or in YMCA foreign secretary Frank H. Wood's refusal to take passage for India with working-class sailors. Both professed disgust at these men's sexual habits and profanity, and acted as if unmitigated contact would leave them contaminated."[16] Contact with moral degenerates was bad for us, for such contact could infect us.

In conclusion, we do not masturbate alone. That is because our bodies remain sites of social interaction, even in private.

Among other things, masturbation is an act of social defiance. The *Seinfeld* episode "The Contest," in which four friends bet on who can "hold out" the longest, drove this point home to the American public. In *Natural Symbols,* the anthropologist Mary Douglas maintains that, since "the human body is always treated as an image of society," there consequently "can be no natural way of considering the body that does not involve at the same time a social dimension."[17] We owe our neighbors a certain standard of conduct they themselves may actively be violating. "Do as I say and not as I do" indeed.

Sado-masochism and Voluntary Slavery

Increasingly often, young Americans graduate from fine colleges without a clue about what to do with their lives. Woody Allen included in the 1986 hit film *Hannah and Her Sisters* an intelligent but shiftless young woman, casting about for a life plan while studying at Barnard. This character no doubt resonates with many Ivy League graduates. Today, plenty of university teachers recognize this character's plight in their own students.

In 1999, two Australian philosophers offered a bold solution for unemployment, a solution that would probably disarm restless "Gen Xers" in America. Ian Hunt and Rodney Allen suggested that voluntary slavery would give unemployed people a purpose in life, and save taxpayers money. You would agree to become a slave in return for lifelong board and lodgings. Once you'd made that contract, you would forfeit your rights to freedom. As I'll discuss shortly, some women may take the view that this is what the institution of marriage long amounted to for wives.

The philosophers reasoned that roughly thirty per cent of the Australian work force faced a lifetime of fairly low-paid casual work and that economic insecurity would plague these unfortunates. Anyone who signed up to be a slave would enjoy the security of lifelong sustenance; slaves, these philosophers reasoned, would even share in the recreations and the life-styles of their wealthy owners. Rights to uninterrupted food supply, lodging and medical care could be guaranteed by a sort of industry regulator. Allen argued, "We, the rest of the people in society could set up—well in the same way as we now have a Royal Society for the Prevention of Cruelty to Animals, and a Royal Society for the Prevention of Cruelty to Children, we could have a royal society for the prevention of cruelty to slaves which would monitor the situation and make sure that slave owners, or prompt the government to make sure that slave owners were meeting their obligations."[18]

Voluntary slavery will strike even harried Gen Xers as bad career advice. Even the most liberal philosophers, those intent on allowing as much individual liberty as possible, have winced at the idea that someone would voluntarily choose to throw away his liberty. Addictions to sex, drugs, or pornography would seem to amount to this, though, as would joining a convent or paying a dominatrix to imprison and torture you. What's the big deal?

In Hegel's *Philosophy of Right* (1821) we find an example of the Enlightenment philosophical consensus that enslaving oneself is not a permissible political liberty. We have a right over our own personality and to an inner life. This right is, for Hegel inalienable: we simply cannot give it away.[19] Voluntary slavery competes with suicide as the worst thing we can do to ourselves.

Many Western philosophers whose arguments now consti-tute the bedrock of our common morality would have objected to sado-masochism. Paul Theroux's 1998 *New Yorker* article "Nurse Wolf" described the livelihood of a young woman born into an affluent Texas family and educated at elite schools. Living in New York City, she supports herself by humiliating male clients in a variety of fashions.[20] Helping men who want to suffer (minor) mental and physical harm, she claims to enjoy her work immensely. Theroux's article derives much of its

punch from the supposedly burgeoning popularity of domina-
trices, women who hire themselves out as bullies and treat men
as slaves. What are we to make of men who employ women to
enslave them, even if only for a day? (a week? a year?)

According to Hegel, we would cease to treat others as persons at all if we regarded them as having the right to sell themselves into slavery. Hegel later says in the same work that slaves
have no duties because they have no rights, and vice versa (he
explicitly says that "religious duties are not here in point").
Slaves can always count on the "absolute right" to free themselves (§66A); like anyone else, a slave enjoys "eternal human
rights." Later, Hegel writes:

> It is in the nature of the case that a slave has an absolute right to
> free himself and that if anyone has prostituted his ethical life by
> hiring himself to thieve and murder, this is an absolute nullity
> and everyone has a warrant to repudiate this contract. The same
> is the case if I hire my religious feeling to a priest who is my con-
> fessor, for such an inward matter a man has to settle with himself
> alone. A religious feeling which is partly in control of someone
> else is no proper religious feeling at all. The spirit is always one
> and single and should dwell in me. I am entitled to the union of
> my potential and my actual being. (p. 241)

This line of reasoning would seem to put in tension mercenaries
who hire themselves out to fight for other nations (the early
American government certainly made use of them in the
American Revolution). Also worthy of note is the sharp disapproval of some form of religious expression. The image of the
confessor triggers thoughts of Roman Catholicism, which has
always insisted on the necessity of confessing sin not directly
(and privately) to God but through a priest. It is not hard
to figure out what Hegel would have said about voluntary
entry into religious orders, with their vows of silence, chastity,
obedience, and poverty. (Hegel seems to view religion as an exclusively private matter; this recognizably Protestant view con-

trasts with Catholic and Jewish theology, both of which empha-
size the role of community in achieving salvation.)

What does Hegel's logic make of work? Can it be said that
we metaphorically sell ourselves into slavery when we take a
job? Certainly this was the case for the vast majority of workers in Victorian England. Marx took up this matter and argued
that most workers amount to a "wage slave."

In *On Liberty* (1859), Mill described the antislavery contract position as limiting a person's "power of voluntarily disposing of his own lot in life." He considered such a contract an
infringement of liberty:

> In this and most other civilized countries . . . an engagement by
> which a person should sell himself, or allow himself to be sold,
> as a slave would be null and void, neither enforced by law nor by
> opinion. The ground for thus limiting his power of voluntarily
> disposing of his own lot in life is apparent, and is very clearly
> seen in this extreme case.[21]

Mill proceeds to defend the nonenforcement of slavery contracts on the ground that this interference with a person's liberty is for the sake of that same person's liberty; respect for
liberty does not require that we allow a person to abdicate liberty. This position of Mill's has been taken to be an exception
to his well-known opposition to the state (or anyone for that
matter) dictating what we must do. Those unwilling to embrace strong paternalism have been forced to seek other justifications for the law's refusal to enforce slavery contracts.[22]

This proscription of selling ourselves into slavery takes on
added significance, given the arguments by some feminist
thinkers (such as Andrea Dworkin and Catherine MacKin-
non) that the institution of marriage enslaves women. Although I do not entirely agree with this view of matrimony, it
is certainly worth noting. Other relevant issues cry out for
mention here—strictures against owning property, against divorce, against inheriting, against working outside the home,

against sexual "laxness." Child custody issues. Women and marriage in India or Nigeria today, say, for example, stoning! We can see that in a variety of cultures traditional marriage combines and reflects discrete social pressures on women: pressure to bear children for status; need for purification rituals after menstruation and childbirth; oppressive mourning customs for widows. It is not hard to see how marriage, like the convent, might feel like slavery.

It is also worth emphasizing that religious devotion has long been viewed as a kind of voluntary slavery (one that nonbelievers will say degrades individuals). Early Christians liked to speak of themselves as "slaves of Christ"; modern sensibilities will sometimes prompt in college classrooms or informal dialogues the question of whether deciding to follow an organized religion differs much from selling oneself into slavery.

Entering a Roman Catholic convent or monastery has inspired lay Catholics and puzzled non-Catholics. Why would anyone choose to take vows of poverty, obedience, and chastity? A more interesting question is, why has Western culture smiled on the ancient monastic system while condemning the idea that individuals have the right to sell themselves into slavery? The idea of voluntary slavery, like philosophical opposition to it, whisks us to the front lines of the battle for personal freedom. Even the most liberal of political philosophers will recoil in horror from the idea than an individual should do such a thing to him or herself.

Most of us will cringe at devotion or altruism that threatens to backfire and make a well-meaning person regret his or her actions. Extreme altruism resembles voluntary slavery. Mr. Zell Kravinsky of Philadelphia did not enter a monastery or indenture himself to the wealthy (he is himself quite wealthy); he chose instead to donate one of his kidneys to a total stranger.[23] His wife, a psychiatrist, threatened to divorce him. His parents denounced the act of their forty-eight-year-old son, who had already given over 45 million dollars to charity. What troubled Kravinsky's family most of all was his stated interest in giving away his other kidney as well. Were he to do so, Kravinky, the father of four children, would die. Kidney donations to strangers are relatively rare in the United States, where 134 such cases have arisen since 1998, according to the United Network for Organ Sharing. Perhaps most remarkable of all is the fact that less than half of Americans who could donate their organs at death do so. The tug between selflessness and selfishness compels most of us to exercise unusual caution.

Prostitution

Without clients, prostitutes would fail. Laws prohibiting prostitution have often focused on the harm prostitutes do to themselves, largely ignoring the harm their clients do to themselves.

A few facts: Sometimes referred to as "the world's oldest profession," prostitution most usually involves a female sex worker and a male client. The female is usually of an age when fertility is assumed, although many prepubescent girls also work as prostitutes. The male client—the john—is usually an adult. Male prostitutes include both fully grown men—presumably still young enough to be considered attractive—and boys. The clients of male prostitutes are also usually male.

Just as those who violate speed limits may be sent to traffic school, so johns are sometimes sent to "John School." Women working as undercover cops ferret out and arrest men who solicit prostitutes. In 2001, the city of Washington, D.C. conformed its "John School" to one in San Francisco: On his first arrest, each man may pay $300 to attend a day of lectures about the consequences of his actions. If he agrees, the city will dismiss his case and the john will avoid both court and a criminal record.[24] Prostitution is not a victimless crime, the educators stress, and johns in Washington, D.C. should celebrate the fact that their pictures are not posted on the Internet, as is done in St. Paul, Minnesota. The Washington authorities averaged nearly forty arrests a month in the first year of their work. The crimes for which johns are held guilty are twofold: exposing themselves to the risk of venereal disease, and victimizing women caught up in a cycle of drug abuse and selling their bodies. (In many societies throughout history, female prostitution has been blamed on the inability of women to control their sexual appetites.) In Washington, most johns are married men whose wives never learn of their arrest.

We are not allowed to rent or sell our bodies: legal and religious sanctions prohibit us from doing so. Starving college students may enroll in medical experiments for cash, but only after they have signed a consent form that makes clear the risks involved. It is hard to imagine that anyone enjoys serving as a guinea pig for medical experiments or working as a streetwalker. When it comes to rights, however, our pleasure does not usually bear on outcomes. Think of gay and lesbian people serving in the military: Why would anyone petition for the right to be shot at? Pleasure is not the deciding factor. Although this book concerns losing control *and* liking it, a brief consideration of prostitution is in order for the reason that so much discussion of harm to the self has focused on it. It seems unlikely to me that many prostitutes enjoy their work, which usually involves losing control over their lives and sometimes their lives altogether (thanks largely to crime and AIDS). A memorable fictive exception here is Luis Buñuel's 1967 film *Belle de Jour,* in which a stunningly beautiful Catherine Deneuve plays a married bourgeoise who enjoys her secret life in a Parisian brothel. She feels liberated from being frightened of sex, from her Roman Catholicism, from her gentility.

The rebellious spirit of *Belle de Jour* thrives in the age of technology. Many people, men and women both, enjoy being admired and directed by faceless strangers in on-line video rooms. The Internet poses a challenge to the traditional formulation of prostitution. In 1995 a lone ranger named Jennifer Ringley hooked up a video camera in her Dickinson College (Pennsylvania) dorm room and allowed the world to watch her go about domestic chores and pastimes.[25] Remarkably, her www.jennicam.org Web site received more than 500,000 "hits" a day. When she later took an apartment in Washington, D.C., she carried the camera with her and continued to allow strangers to watch her sleeping, working, or even cavorting with her boyfriend in bed—for a yearly fee of fifteen dollars (she created a nonprofit organization out of the Web site).[26]

It's hard to tell the difference between the Jennicam and the porn industry, and mainstream entertainment increasingly uses soft core material. All the world's a stage. This "Jennicam" idea / Web site has mushroomed, and now other private citizens allow strangers to watch them, voyeuristically. What if a person were to charge access to her Web site, which would feature live footage of her sexually stimulating herself? Selling yourself to viewers you cannot see (and who cannot touch you or find out where you live) might well be considered a purely self-regarding form of prostitution. Let me entertain you.

What about old-fashioned stripping: Does it constitute prostitution? Columbia University graduate Elisabeth Eaves has argued in a provocative memoir that her stripping job ought to be considered something quite different from prostitution. After graduating from college, she wilted in low-paying secretarial jobs in Seattle. When she discovered she could make significantly more money stripping and, at the same time, get the chance to show off the body of which she was so proud, she launched a new career. She believed that her body mesmerized men, that she could manipulate them with it, even render them powerless. She saw herself as being in control. She emphasized that strippers do not lack free will—they are not coerced into the profession. She discovered that the wall between watching and touching made a world of moral difference to her, and she did not allow men to touch her. "It wasn't the act itself, it was a matter of setting up boundaries *somewhere,* so that one didn't feel like one's entire self was oozing away."[27] Anyone insisting that Eaves was fooling herself in denying she worked as a prostitute should remember that stripping enjoys legal status in the state of Washington, where she worked, but prostitution does not. How much difference is there between Eaves and the waitresses in the Hooters chain of restaurants? Hooters—like Playboy bunnies long before them —wear tight-fitting, low-cut blouses on the job, as well as "hotpants." How do we classify them?

Prostitution in various forms has angered upstanding citizens of different cultures and epochs. With only one exception, all American states prohibit prostitution as a crime; the outlier, Nevada, delegates the decision to the county. State criminal laws define prostitution variously as selling sex (reaching wholly private conduct) or soliciting the sale of sex (focusing on prostitution as a public nuisance). Some, but not all, of the states also make patronizing a prostitute a crime, although nowhere are patrons prosecuted in the same numbers or with the same vigor as prostitutes. All of the states also make it a crime for third parties to profit from prostitution, including business agents (pimps), solicitors (panderers), recruiters, and those who rent real estate for the purposes of prostitution.

Bad for us: The fully voluntary choice of an adult woman to work as a prostitute, and the choice of an adult man to patronize her. Criminalizing these choices curtails the liberty of both parties. We have long justified intervention into economic relationships by telling ourselves that prostitutes despise their labor. However, it is not especially difficult to find sex workers who assert that sexual prostitution seems no better or worse than other, socially legitimate jobs they have held.[28] Xaviera Hollander titillated many with her tales of a "happy hooker." Later came the revelations of "Mayflower Madam" Sydney Biddle Barrows. More recently, the American performance artist Annie Sprinkle has written of enjoying her work as a prostitute. Men as well have enjoyed prostitution: Alan Helms writes candidly of his happy days being kept in Park Avenue apartment by a French nobleman in the book *Young Man from the Provinces*. I remain somewhat skeptical of these accounts.

Various scholars have favored decriminalizing adult, consensual prostitution, removing all criminal laws (including those against soliciting, patronizing, or living off the earnings of a prostitute).[29] These authors generally propose regulating sex commerce through existing labor laws, protecting prostitutes as workers, and treating pimps and patrons as employers. Prostitution would be a legal labor contract, subject to the civil and administrative penalties already applicable to, for example, child or sweatshop labor. A patron or pimp who makes an arrangement for prostitution would be penalized like the employer who seeks to employ underage workers in unsafe working conditions or at rates below minimum wage. Legal scholars Linda Hirshman and Jane Larson have argued that treating prostitution as socially undesirable labor is the best response to an activity that fits uncomfortably into our pluralistic scheme of values.

Libertarians, including a feminist wing, generally favor the legalization of prostitution; they tie criminalization to vestiges of Christian revulsion and fears of female promiscuity. They favor making sexual services available to the general public in the same way that food and shelter are. A closely related position, most powerfully advanced by prostitutes on their own behalf, is that criminalizing the sex trade unfairly restricts women's economic opportunities (this is Elisabeth Eaves's position in *Bare*). Selling sex is among the highest paid of female occupations, and women should be allowed to use their bodies and labor to greatest personal advantage. Illegality arguably reinforces entrenched traditions by which, throughout Western history, other people have controlled female sexuality.

Regardless of laws prohibiting it, prostitution remains an option for both women and men to earn money. The idea of raising a family through funds raised in this way will strike many as abhorrent; it is the human side of prostitution that bothers us. Despite first-person narratives by sex workers who claim that their work isn't so bad, it seems unlikely that many prostitutes enjoy their work more than do people working in factories or prisons.

The short story "The Art of Eating" usefully deepens the important question of how exactly to define prostitution. In the story a sixty-year-old woman named Bobbie Lake moves in with an old man who, once in love with food, is now too ill to eat.[30] The man orders Bobbie to eat rich and exotic foods and to describe every morsel. "She knew her body was being bought . . . But Bobbie didn't care at last, because she'd thought her body too old for wanting. And here some wrecked old fellow had found parts of her still alive." The provocative story suggests a compassionate side to prostitution (although pure compassion would likely rule out the exchange of money for the service provided). Getting ahead in school or at the office, among various other demands of ordinary life, may lead us to prostitute ourselves metaphorically.

As I have indicated, some thinkers view sex workers as legitimate professionals, not so unlike other laborers who draw a salary for completing manual labor. Whether or not prostitutes derive emotional satisfaction from their trade matters little here (it is a relatively modern idea, the vision of work as a means of self-fulfillment): The question at hand is whether we can say that sex workers harm themselves through their work. It does not seem obvious that consenting adult workers engaged in safe-sex practices do harm to themselves. (On the other hand, it is also obvious that nonconsenting adults, or adults driven into prostitution solely out of economic need, or child prostitutes, or workers engages in unsafe sex practices are in great danger of harming themselves emotionally and physically. The third world has a severe problem in this area, and the first world is by no means immune from it either.)

Televised Humiliation

Many people live in fear of humiliating themselves. The idea of giving a speech to a large audience, singing a solo in church, or striking out at bat will keep them hiding in the privacy of their homes. "Nothing ventured, nothing gained," we might shake our heads and say of them. And yet we understand the pay-off of their strategy.

Other people seem to run to opportunities to make fools of themselves. They want the microphone at wedding celebrations, so they can sing something. The "class clown" wants to heckle the teacher at school, even at the risk of having to stand silently in the corner. The "life of the party" reaches for the proverbial lampshade, to place on his head. And some will run from one disastrous love affair to another. Making a fool of ourselves needn't involve a crowd but often does.

In the event others do see us humiliate ourselves, we become small-scale celebrities. That is, after all, part of the reason we decline opportunities to sing solos and give speeches. Our failures will live on longer in the memory of witnesses than we'd like. The difference between us and proper celebrities lies in the crowds who laugh at us or faint before us.

The cult of celebrity induces swooning. Teenagers may be chastised for giddily trembling over a rock singer or movie star. Parents don't want their children to appear fools, and so adults may urge emotional restraint on kids who revel in the emotional abandon of swooning, a form of silliness.

It's by no means just teenagers who swoon, though. Non-Catholics sometimes puzzle at the notion of making a pilgrimage to see the foot, finger, or face of a saint long dead. Non-Catholic tourists in European churches will sometimes regard the behavior of the faithful who find themselves in the presence of a holy relic as swooning. This spiritual abandon or devotion can lead to drastic ends. We now cringe when we see film footage of Hitler riding through German crowds. His supporters lean forward, gasp, and reach out to him. They yearn to be in his presence and seem to dissolve in ecstatic tremors. Saints, rock stars, Hitler. The historian Peter Gay writes that in the nineteenth century, performances of Wagner's opera *Tristan und Isolde* (1865) "made Wagner's munificent patron, King Ludwig II of Bavaria, literally swoon."[31] Gay quotes a German musicologist, who recalled that "on all countenances" one could "see the expression of the greatest emotion." Many were "weeping passionately"; not just "nervous ladies," rhapsodic and lyrical, but "serious men had tears in their eyes." A young American in the audience "was trembling so convulsively that he had to be removed to get some fresh air." Anyone in the theater who had a heart, it seemed, surrendered to gushing emotion while listening to Wagner. Throwing personal pride to the wind, upstanding citizens yelped.

Swooning resembles camp humor, the zany laughs raised in Mel Brooks films or saccharine melodramas. Both swooning and camp involve refusals—in swooning, we pay too much homage and in camp, we fail to pay sufficient respect. In the history of twentieth-century humor, many Jewish and gay entertainers deflected attention away from the fact of their Jewishness or gayness by means of camp. They played the clown and mocked themselves in order to distract others from noticing what really threatened their membership in society at large. Take, for example, the American popular entertainer Liberace, who regularly had so much fun laughing at himself with his over-the-top, yet likeable outfits and mannerisms that it was virtually impossible to make fun of him. He always beat us to the punch.

There is a difference between purposively seeking to humiliate ourselves and noting with approval or perhaps even pleasure that we have been humiliated. At the end of Verdi's opera *Falstaff* (1893), an adaptation of Shakespeare's *Merry Wives of Windsor*, the Falstaff has been made a fool of. He deserved to have it done; he had misbehaved. But, surrounded by the laughing crowd, a couple of whom have also been bested for their own faults, Falstaff lovingly pronounces: "The whole world is a joke, and man's born a clown." The crowd agrees and everyone joins in singing with the fat knight.

*　　*　　*

A PECULIAR FORM OF SWOONING HAS EMERGED IN THE
United States: baring one's intimate secrets on a nationally
televised talk show. We can make a circus of our private lives
and enjoy brief fame as a reward. Yale sociologist Joshua Gamson sat in the audiences of talk shows in different American
cities and interviewed twenty production staff members and
forty-four guests. He concluded that guests on talk shows "do
considerable damage to themselves and others."[32]

Talk show guinea pigs receive free airfare and a hotel room
in New York, Los Angeles, or Chicago, a bit of television exposure, a shot of attention and a microphone, and some
free "therapy." In exchange, guests publicly air their fetishes,
their troubles with relationships, and their embarrassing experiences, usually in the manner most likely to grab ratings:
exaggerated, loud, and oversimplified. Citizens who feel mar-
ginalized or who cannot afford or imagine therapy are most
vulnerable to the seduction of television. As critics suggest,
talk shows do not offer an ideal arrangement for guests, since
bruiting problems in front of an audience cannot substitute
for actually working them out. The very idea of getting help
from public confession would seem wrong-headed: Sociologist
Vicki Abt has said that telling secrets on television is "like defe-
cating in public."[33]

Why would anyone harm him or herself in this way? On
television talk shows, guests often say, you feel appreciated.
You are begged and coached and applauded to tell your very
own story in front of millions of people. You feel special, even
important. In fact, though, you become a circus sideshow.[34]

Talk shows are show business, and it is their mission to ex-
ploit. They commodify and manipulate confessions to build
an entertainment product, which is then used to attract audiences, who then are sold to advertisers, which results in a profit
for the producers. Exploitation thus ought to be the starting
point for analysis and not, as it so often is, its conclusion. Al-

lowing ourselves to be exploited for mass entertainment indicates poor judgment. It seems reasonable to conclude that many talk show guests will suffer from regret.

Publicized humiliation or embarrassment would seem to be in even greater vogue now, at least in the United States and in other parts of the world as well. The popularity of the talk shows has in some part contributed to the creation of the MTV show *Real World,* in which college-age people of varying demographic backgrounds agree to be confined within a house and filmed at random. The CBS television show *Survivor* captivated America in the year 2000: The allure of watching real people "trapped" on a desert island as they decide how far to compromise their dignity in the name of survival skyrocketed the ratings of this program. Having watched O. J. Simpson flee police on the Los Angeles highway, the beating of Rodney King, the surging airplane of golf champion Payne Stewart destined to crash and burn, and the sexual assaults of various young women in broad daylight in Central Park, modern consumers have demonstrated a hunger for verisimilitude. Humiliation in a play or a film no longer suffices; we have to see it really happening to an actual person.

Kant would strenuously object to the idea of offering up one's dignity for the entertainment of others. A whole genre of children's stories aims to inculcate good sense in the leaders of tomorrow. Television talk shows overturn the sensibility of lessons children learn through early books. Later, morality plays or cautionary tales serve the same purpose: to remind adults that foolishness can usher in an excruciating realization. Others will have a hard time humiliating us unless we cooperate. Poor judgment, no less than pride, goeth before the fall.

Posing Naked for the Camera

We've already considered the moral classification of strippers working in clubs and exhibitionists living in front of Internet cameras. What about people who never intend for public consumption the photographs they pose for and home movies they star in? We have no way of knowing how many of our neighbors or colleagues guard nude photographs of themselves, but the Internet bulges with such images.

Where else but the Internet can you turn for an honest opinion of how your breasts or penis look? Entire Web sites are devoted to helping you find the answer. After all, friends will only give you a biased appraisal. But if you post shots of the delicate areas on the right Web site, an endless parade of amateur critics can rate your assets. They can leave comments for you too. At your convenience you can check the site to see how you're faring. Web sites make gathering such information much easier; very few Americans will ever get a chance to appear on the "reality" television show *Are You Hot?*, which exists to provide the same sort of feedback (as it is not exactly a pornographic show, it can't actually picture the goods, so to speak).

In a new camcorder era, more and more people are recording their amateur strip shows. More and more people are allowing themselves to be videotaped in bedroom scenarios. In years to come, more and more of these photographs and videotapes will reach the public (think of the radio talk show host Dr. Laura Schlessinger and the heiress Paris Hilton). What will we make of the fact that celebrities, politicians, and even clergy are starring in bawdy scripts of their own devising?

Vanessa Williams, the first black woman ever to be named Miss America (in 1983), relinquished her title in 1984, after nude photographs of her emerged. Not only had she posed naked, she had frolicked with another naked woman while doing so. (*Penthouse* published a series of these photos in 1984.) Not long afterward, actor Rob Lowe was publicly pilloried for having allowed himself to be videotaped while in bed with other naked people (including an underage girl). In the late 1990s, an African-American man named Christian Curry sued the Wall Street firm Morgan Stanley Dean Witter for unfair dismissal and racism. Curry, a recent graduate of Columbia University, had posed naked and in a state of prominent arousal before joining the corporate world. When photo spreads of the young investment banker appeared in two different magazines for gay men, Curry's career careened. His employer insisted publicly that Curry had been fired because of expense account fraud, while Curry alleged racism and homophobia (even though Curry claimed to be heterosexual, he alleged that his inclusion in magazines targeted at gay men led to the widespread assumption that he himself was gay). Curry sued Morgan Stanley, and the New York tabloids had a field day.

A similar lawsuit arose in North Carolina in 2002. The winner of the Miss North Carolina pageant, Rebekah Revels, was pressured to step down once nude photographs of her came to light. According to section 1g of the contest rules, a contestant must be "of good moral character" and must never have engaged "in any activity which could be characterized as dishonest, immoral, immodest, indecent, or in bad taste." A new Miss North Carolina, Misty Clymer, was named, but Revels took her case to court, alleging that the photographs had been taken by her boyfriend and against her will.[35] The images fell into the wrong hands, much as the notorious videotape of the celebrities Pamela Anderson and Tommy Lee did (the two had filmed themselves having sex). The court decided to reinstate Revels, and North Carolina was represented by not one but two women in the Miss America pageant later that fall.

Perhaps the most interesting incident of this sort surfaced in 2002 as well. In a curious twist on the traditional Oedipal script, a son publicly circulated hundreds of naked photographs of his deceased father, who had been a minor television star in the 1960s and 1970s. Scotty Crane, the son of "sex addict" Bob Crane, who had starred in the television series *Hogan's Heroes,* claimed great pride in the erotic escapades of his father, along with the record of those escapades left by his father.[36] When a mass-market film entitled *Auto Focus* was released on the subject of Bob Crane's penchant for filming himself having sex with a parade of different women, Scotty Crane fought a public battle with his half-brother Bobby Crane. Bobby insisted that Scotty was only trying to profit financially from publicizing his father's sexual athleticism. The story of Bob, Scotty, and Bobby Crane underscored how compelling bad behavior could be. The idea of a son taking public pleasure in the genital size and sexual prowess of his philandering father registered a new note on the American scale of celebrity fascination.

We can expect a stream of naked photographs and videotapes to compromise the careers of public figures in years to come. It would seem prudent for public figures or people with aspirations to fame to withstand the temptation to pose for the camera in a way that may come back to haunt, but this advice may be asking too much of contemporary Westerners, particularly those with beautiful bodies.

Of course, if American mores were to change, posing nude for the camera would cease to be politically dangerous, bad for us. In a clever public relations move in 1985, the American singer Madonna responded to the news that photographs of her taken years earlier would soon appear in *Playboy* magazine. She announced that she would be publishing her own collection of naked shots. By refusing to feel ashamed, Madonna compelled Americans to congratulate her for having a genuinely beautiful body. Madonna reminded America that what made her special was an energetic naughtiness, a hunger for what is bad for us. Madonna knew that she could sustain an entire career on the back of our own thirst for stories of people doing what is bad for them.

In a historic recall election, California voters chose Arnold Schwarzenegger their new governor in October 2003. He is probably the first U.S. governor to have posed in the nude (you can find pictures on the Internet easily, and as well as numerous peek-a-boo shots throughout the documentary *Pumping Iron*). How is it that Miss North Carolina lost her title (however temporarily) but Schwarzenegger won the election? Is it all right for a man to pose naked, but not a woman? Or do the Miss America pageant judges simply hold higher moral standards than California voters? Nudity can still jolt Americans, which explains why artists such as Matthew Barney and Karen Finley disrobe to such notorious effect.

If there is any real danger here, it is that celebrity candidates and aspiring artists will start circulating nude shots of themselves to increase publicity, and having a beautiful body will become one of the criteria by which voters and audiences decide their loyalty. When New Jersey politicians tried to heap shame on Democratic candidate Jim Morrison in 2003 for having entered two "Prettiest Penis" contests in the mid-1990s, he simply informed voters that he had won, both times.

Hanging Out

Our bosses hate the thought that we may secretly coast through our days. We only work when someone is looking, they fear. Just as our bosses want us to "work, work, work!," so does Kant. Whereas our bosses want us to make them richer, Kant wants us to make ourselves nobler. Kant tells us that we must work to become all that we can.

Kant calls it a moral duty to develop our talents. This amounts to something quite a bit more important than the medieval classification of sloth as one of the seven deadly sins. Few modern writers have noticed or cared to pick up on the *moral obligation* to cultivate our minds and characters. Harold Bloom's book *How to Read and Why* comes close.[37] Bloom declares in his introduction that reading is "the most healing of pleasures"; it returns us "to otherness" and yet also makes us "wholly ourselves." For Bloom, reading canonical authors or works of moral philosophy amounts to one of the best ways not only to spend our time but to develop ourselves. "Only deep, constant reading fully establishes and augments an autonomous self," Bloom counsels. The written word makes the man.

Meanwhile, soccer moms and swimming dads cart their kids off to endless practices and lessons. Parents strive to expose their children to ballet, bowling, and basketball. Particularly in America, parents are given to hope that their children possess some extraordinary skill. They have come to feel entitled to the fame that comes from some sort of excellence.

In any event, we are not supposed to lounge about the house as an idle millionaire, watching MTV, and eating potato chips all day long. If we take Kant seriously, then indulging our inclination to relaxation after a hard week in the office or at school borders on harming ourselves. Recharging our battery is one thing, but frittering away precious time another.

Alas, for all of his extraordinary insight, Kant failed to appreciate women. He did not consider them capable of much intellectual achievement, much less of moral deliberation. Indeed, he did not consider them intelligent enough to do more than meet the material needs of children. What should today's well-educated young woman do as she wrestles with the desire to forgo a demanding and potentially quite lucrative career in favor of staying at home to raise children with a man who goes to work to pay the bills? Such a young woman may well worry about the creative and professional potential she is sacrificing (even if only temporarily).

Kant's thinking will hardly inspire women. Times have changed dramatically, and millions of Western women now feel the burden from which Kant inadvertently shielded them: to develop their talents. In the course of meeting this moral duty, modern women struggle to balance their professional and personal responsibilities. How to be a career mom dominates the columns of numerous women's magazines and preoccupies some of the more interesting philosophers, sociologists, and psychologists of our day.

Professional women aside, the so-called duty to develop personal potential remains a morally complicated matter, as I will argue in chapter nine. Liberated moderns, especially in America, may insist until their last breath that they should have the moral right to do whatever they like with their free time. Should they wish to spend every weekend on the couch watching professional sports or MTV, so be it. And yet we tell ourselves a story in which we can become and accomplish anything we want. According to the Horatio Alger myth, every kid can go to Harvard. And should, it sometimes seems. Ambitious parents, convinced their children possess enormous potential, push their children to achieve, achieve, achieve.

The idea that we all possess some gorgeous potential masks a romantic ideal. Children living in poverty often achieve very little, apart from survival. We hate to see adults living in poverty, but we feel even worse when we see children in dire straits. Why is that? Destitute adults squandered their chances, we may tell ourselves (even though we don't quite know what those imaginary chances were). Maybe that's why they're poor now—because they didn't work hard enough to realize their potential. But when it comes to children, we understand viscerally that there are no chances of which to speak. That realization scares us.

In our particularly charitable moments, we like to think that poor children could become Olympic champions or Pulitzer Prize winners. In those moments, we rarely consider the possibility that, given lots of chances, poor children might end up like our children: given to lying on the couch in front of the television.

To be sure, there is a difference between lassitude (lying in front of the television all day) and not developing our talents (because we are spending all of out time ferrying our children from one rehearsal to another lesson, or because of involuntary unemployment). Had Kant respected women more, he would have perhaps lamented how child-raising responsibilities (to take just one example) usually fall to women. It is much easier to blame laziness. While emotions seem to loom behind many of the ways we harm ourselves, emotions have little if anything to do with languor. For where there is emotion, there is arousal.

Slothful people may or may not enjoy their inactivity—it is hard to say. However, psychiatrists worry about them. People who claim that their lives have no purpose and that therefore there is no point to making an effort at much of anything are often depressed. In extreme cases of depression, suicide may become appealing. Despair certainly does not qualify as the eventual result of sloth, for the vast majority of slothful people do manage to get something done. It's just that they could do much more with their lives, critics say, if only they got to work. Regret must surely hound them, we think, because of all that they've missed. Of course, the slothful may tell us that they're not missing anything: Television watching or Internet surfing is precisely what they want. Some of them may really succeed at holding their self-worth apart from their achievements.

Sloth fills out and deepens the notion of harming the self. Usually we think of people who lack self-control as impulsive and inclined to say or do rash things. It might well seem that the slothful lack motivation, though, not self-control. If we think of self-discipline as part of self-control, however, then we can make sense of the claim that lazy people harm themselves. Lie-abouts can't resist doing nothing in the way that other transgressors can't resist whatever it is that we insist harms them. The whole point of examining particular ways in which we supposedly harm ourselves is to develop a sense for the distinctiveness of losing self-control as a moral experience.

Of course, an inability to thrive, a failure to succeed, may come down to factors that have nothing to do with laziness. But a workaholic culture will naturally scorn "lie-abouts." On some level, it doesn't matter so much *what* people do ("All work is honorable," according to an old saying) as *that* they do something. What tops the *Harvard Business Review*'s list of essential qualities for success in business? "A high level of drive and energy." This business prerequisite seems to be a moral one as well.

Drug Use

If quilters and stamp collectors form clubs, why shouldn't narcotics users? Notable French writers such as Victor Hugo, Alexander Dumas, Théophile Gautier, and Charles Baudelaire formed a club in the nineteenth century, Le Club des Hachichins. These writers gathered to sing the praises of cannabis, which they claimed enhanced their creativity. Psychopharmacological dalliances can make us feel terrific, yet mind-altering drugs remain illegal in many countries.

Whether hallucinogens, inebriants, hypnotics, or narcotics, contraband substances arouse widespread social disapproval. The Harrison Act of 1914 not only established drug prohibition in the U.S. but also provided a model for other Western countries to follow suit.

On November 5, 1996, residents of California and Arizona voted overwhelmingly to legalize marijuana for medical use. Mike Gray has detailed this stunning defeat for prohibitionists.[38] Both Proposition 200 in Arizona and Proposition 215 in California allowed medical patients to use marijuana virtually without limit, but the Arizona voters went further, turning the clock back eighty years to a time when doctors could prescribe any drug they saw fit, including heroin.

Gray reports that six days before the vote, a letter signed by three former presidents exhorted voters to keep marijuana illegal; some leaders wanted voters to avoid sending "the erroneous message that dangerous and addictive drugs such as heroin, LSD, marijuana and methamphetamine are safe." However, the electorate responded more positively to television commercials explaining how marijuana can help cancer patients cope with the nausea, vomiting, and loss of appetite that come with chemotherapy.

Of course, there is an important difference between using contraband drugs to escape pain and to seek pleasure. The voters in Arizona and California saw themselves acting compassionately, helping sick people find relief from terrible pain. Psychiatrists will tell us, though, that many recreational drug users are fleeing pain as well. The stress of day-to-day life, keeping up with responsibilities, and stomaching our own failures may, on balance, feel every bit as bad as physical pain. Who's to say only the physically ill should be entitled to relief?

Drug addicts differ from recreational drug users. By definition, addicts do not enjoy losing control. They have no control to lose. In contrast, recreational use again poses the question of whether it can make sense, if indeed it does, to plan a temporary loss of control. If so, then it does make sense to speak of recreational, occasional drug use. Some drugs leave behind an unforgettably pleasant memory that leads people to seek out that experience again compulsively. Psychological dependence on caffeine, alcohol, or tobacco bothers few, but hard-core drug addicts bother many. Addicts are considered unwholesome individuals unwilling or incapable of controlling their own selfish gratification.

The New York critic Ann Marlowe has challenged Western preconceptions of drug abusers, even going so far as to assert that we glamorize drugs by condemning them. She makes the remarkable claim that substances such as heroin, which she took regularly for ten years, cannot addict us unless we want them to. A champion of self-control, she insists that we all have it, and we can all use it. She walked away from heroin without any medical help (medical experts reckon that some two percent of the population can do this), insisting that the problem with drug use is not the drugs, but the people who use them. Generally speaking, we like addiction: "Addiction isn't just a possible outcome, it's a partial motivation for drug use."[39] She asserts that addiction is *not* uncontrollable need (p. 228) and that Western culture is simply wrong. "For some of us, once you realize addiction is out there, you have to try it. Or in any case, once you realize a flirtation with addiction is possible, you have to explore it" (p. 144). Her memoir may flabbergast us, not so much because her conclusions seem counterintuitive, but because it is impossible to disprove her conviction that people come to heroin to find self-control, not to lose it (p. 198). Heroin structures your week and gives you something to look forward to, she maintains, as well as provides you with a sense of being special. She believes that legalizing drugs would remove their "transgressive glamour," such that people would stop using them.

One of the earliest accounts of drug addiction in the West is that by Thomas De Quincey, who published *Confessions of an English Opium-Eater* in 1822 and claimed that the number of "amateur opium-eaters" in London at that time was "immense." The drama of De Quincey's addiction has seduced many, despite the acute sense of loss that may sneak up on any drug user. Contraband substances may rob users of self-control by driving them to distraction and filling them with regret. On a social level, organized crime has mushroomed around the drug trade. While drug use carries people to an outlawed state of altered feelings, drug trafficking raises the risks of narcotics possession to dizzying heights.

Conventional wisdom holds that one of the strongest reasons for prohibiting drugs would be the great number of new users that legality would create. Plenty of people would likely turn to drugs to seek consolation from pain-filled and anxiety-ridden lives. By forbidding people from smoking marijuana in the privacy of their homes (even just in principle), we are telling them that we have their best interest at heart. We are trying to stop them from hurting themselves.

Highly addictive substances such as crack cocaine pose the greatest challenge to the idea that a little revolution every now and then is a good thing. Crack has helped to impoverish many a family and destroy its fabric (child care responsibility, housing upkeep, health maintenance often become lost luxuries for the crack addict). In order to recommend occasional mischief as a kind of moral homeopathy, adventures away from the routine have to be stabilized by the routine itself. But when it is likely that a particular drug will overtake the user's life, then it is hard to make a case even for its occasional use—the occasion will likely become the routine and quite possibly lead to self-destruction. The adventures must be punctuated by routine. (There's an obvious parallel to alcohol, of course. Most people are able to drink without mishap, but some will become drunks.) Because controlled substances such as crack and heroin may come to control us, highly addictive drugs are not a good idea. We cannot pick them up at will and turn on our heels when we like, as Marlowe claims to have done. The price of fun soars too high, when we take into consideration the costs of substance addiction.

Self-neglect

Sins of omission balance sins of commission, and each deserves attention here. I have already mentioned the cost of sloth: not making something of ourselves, or not becoming all that we can be. Here I want to mention a related harm: leading a busy life, a life so busy that we direct outward energy that should be directed inward. Self-neglect often characterizes those who labor in the "helping professions"—nurses, nuns, teachers. We praise people such as these for dedicating their lives in the service of others' welfare. But self-neglect can also happen to the rich and powerful: the businessmen, politicians, and movie stars who become workaholics. In an increasingly hectic world, fewer people have time for themselves.

Allowing frantically busy schedules to drive our daily lives is arguably even worse for us than the torpor that may set in from dull, monotonous work. We may neglect our health, our partners, our friends and family, our appearance, our need for "down time." We may stop reading because we don't have the time. We may settle for junk food meals. We may skip our yearly check-ups. We may lose the ability to sit still. We may lose, at least to some degree, our sense of ourselves as individuals.

In 1969, Theodore Roszak warned us about the psychological toll large corporations would take on those who worked within them. In *The Making of a Counter Culture*, he emphasized self-expression over self-control. The great enemy was technocracy, by which he meant "that social form in which an industrial society reaches the peak of its organizational integration. It is the ideal men usually have in mind when they speak of modernizing, up-dating, rationalizing, planning."[40] Bureaucracy by its very nature, Roszak believed, encourages self-neglect. Like nineteenth-century Romantics before him, he insisted that self-expansion is the purpose of life and encouraged a childlike exuberance. Throughout the twentieth century, more and more social critics rallied behind the familiar message that technology threatened to enslave human beings as the power and shape of corporate America mushroomed at an astonishing rate.

Even outside of work, self-neglect can creep up on us. Our homes are filled with noise we barely register in our inner exhaustion: television, radio, CD players, kids, pets, electronic games, computers. Time passes quickly, and we suddenly realize that we have not heard from ourselves in quite a while. We begin to dream of a quiet vacation away, by ourselves, or with a calmer version of our own family, on a cruise or at a beach or a mountain retreat. We may even think about taking up yoga, meditation, or listening to New Age music.

Self-neglect affects sexual activity. A fatigued inner life means that sexual performance can become routine, or even dwindle away altogether. A mismatched marriage, an ill-advised affair, crass one-night stands, or even a lethargic celibacy can all come out of a state of sustained self-neglect.

Only in the waning years of the twentieth century could public discussion of homosexual self-neglect take place. Certainly gay men and women still stuff themselves into conventional heterosexual marriages. But no longer will they find themselves automatic recipients of sympathy from close friends. No longer must gay men and women resign themselves to sexual boredom. Sexual self-neglect has moved from a simple assumption to an existential worry for a certain segment of contemporary Westerners.

The deathbed offers perhaps the best possible gauge of self-neglect. It's been said that at death's door, no one has been heard to cry, "I wish I'd spent more time at the office!" Whether or not this is so, we can assume that many a dying person has wished he'd spent more time working on a marriage, laughing with his children, helping others, or getting to know himself better. Even the most extroverted person has probably wished, at the end of his or her life, for a little more time to reflect.

Ruling the Self

These, then, are some examples of harm to the self. Surely, there are others. Voluntary self-mutilation, for example, calms some people suffering from stress, even as it worries their friends and families.[41] Burning works too. Changing our sex, surgically acquiring different genitals, continues to elicit social concern. The Reformation theologian John Calvin, to take yet another example, thought that we harm ourselves by not marrying (even today, many Mormons and Muslims would agree).[42] Not surprisingly, traditional religious thinkers often associate harms to the self with divine punishment: Although no earthly tribunal will put you in jail for declining the institution of marriage or exchanging your genitals for others, God will surely see to it that you are punished.

Some harms are admittedly more trivial than others. It can be difficult to rank their gravity: Should refusing to wear a bright shirt while hunting in the forest merit less disapproval than cutting one's arms and legs with a knife after a hard day at the office? Penalties for harming ourselves have largely softened—reading forbidden books or gazing on forbidden images could land our forebears in prison, for example, whereas we see pornography virtually everywhere we turn.

The passage of time makes some worries seem trivial, much as I discussed in chapter one. Criminal excuses play off of moral worries. Ted Bundy, one of the highest-profile mass murderers of the twentieth century, explained shortly before his 1989 electrocution in Florida that pornography had prompted him to kill at least thirty women. A young Republican law student with the face of a movie star and a strong academic record, he blamed his proclivity for rape and murder on porn, which he claimed had significantly harmed him. As criminal excuses go, Bundy's failed to surpass Danny White's. For in the infamous "Twinkie defense," the 1978 murderer of Harvey Milk and San Francisco mayor George Moscone defended himself in court by pleading that junk food had weakened his normally sound judgment. (White, a former city supervisor in San Franciso, had resigned his seat on the board following the enactment of the Gay Civil Rights bill that he had opposed; astonishingly, he was sentenced to a mere seven years and eight months in prison for the double homicide.) By showing us that they agree with prevailing moral principles, criminals can sometimes persuasively renounce their deeds, which violated those same principles. It may even be possible that some criminals *believe* that *they* represent the virtuous high road. Certainly, many fictional serial murderers on TV crime shows profess moral repulsion for the prostitutes they have graphically murdered. Jack the Ripper?

The possibilities for moral disagreement stretch out before us. Although Kant thought that wasting our talents or neglecting our potential excellence was one of the more serious harms we could do ourselves, many Americans will debate whether living as a "couch potato" amounts to harm at all: It should be our prerogative to spend our free time however we like, they will argue. These may be the same people who will insist on the basic right to physician-assisted suicide when faced with a dire medical diagnosis.

The standard of moral excellence is up for grabs, and some philosophers will condemn the medicine that Kant prescribes. In the early twentieth century, the Cambridge University philosopher Bertrand Russell pointed the blame at the sense of sin, in an essay by that very name. Russell argued that religious believers feel irrational guilt over meaningless wrongdoings that affect no one but themselves. To him, the guilt and even misery believers suffer through qualified as one of the greatest harms to the self.

What has interested me here is not the limit on what we may do to others, but on what we may do to or with ourselves. Although others may disapprove, we are free to get peaceably drunk in our homes on weekends. We may not, however, drive a car while drunk, peaceably or otherwise, because we are endangering other people's safety. When we endanger others, they call us negligent, reckless, or criminal. When we endanger ourselves—taking up cliff diving or going on a hunger strike, say—they call us stupid, crazy, or possibly courageous. Depends.

What we take from this discussion of concrete harms to the self is the sense that former no-nos lie closer in history's rearview mirror than we might at first think. Beyond that, a useful contrast emerges between, say, a lie-about and a thrill-seeker. Thrill-seekers and adrenaline groupies, craving the excitement of firsthand experience, rush to roller coasters and hang gliders. Lie-abouts, craving the comforts of secondhand experience, watch twenty-four-hour sports marathons on their living-room TVs instead. To the beat of various drummers, we taste what pleasures we will.

We distrust the hunger for danger, the forbidden, the nonroutine, just as we distrust the desire for complacency. We, each of us, use morality as a weapon of sorts to scare someone else away from doing what he or she intends. We'll see that this is the soil from which raving grows: when people around us pass moral judgments of us based on perceived harm, and on what they think is best for us.

Up to a certain point, most of us can live with a bad conscience. We can judge others' actions without feeling ashamed of ourselves. And we can defy others' judgments without feeling ashamed of ourselves. Whatever our job or home life, we can in fact maintain an effective balance between rebellion and routine, with routine dominant.

chapter four

Protecting Us from Ourselves

WHOSE BUSINESS IS IT HOW WE CHOOSE TO LIVE? PLENTY of people mind our business, whether we are public figures or not. What our communities expect of us morally bears down upon us, just as religious pronouncements about what God expects of us used to do. Over two hundred years ago, the Irish statesman Edmund Burke asserted that each of us has a proper place to stand in; if we step out of line, the world will hold it against us. He thought that each of us enters into a contract of sorts just by living: The world gives us something, and we must give something back. Not an especially religious man, Burke thought that our relation to government mirrored humanity's relation to God. He wrote:

> Each contract of each particular state is but a clause in the great primeval contract of eternal society, linking the lower with the higher natures, connecting the visible and invisible world, according to a fixed compact sanctioned by the individual oath which holds all physical and all moral natures each in their appointed place.[1]

Elsewhere the influential orator asserted that we qualify for civil liberty in exact proportion to our ability to put "moral chains" on our appetites and passions. Burke captures the way many conservatives feel today. Secular moralists as well as religious leaders still urge us to consider what it takes to lead a good life—for example, which foods to avoid, what kinds of sexual activity and entertainment to swear off, and which sensibility to cultivate.

Getting a grip on ourselves is the goal of those who counsel us how to steer the wheel of our own lives. When we muster control of ourselves, we will resist temptation. What does control look like and where does it come from? For many of us, learning to pay attention in school comes as one of the earliest lessons. Later in our education, learning to concentrate on geometry problems or Latin translations gives a vivid sense of what it feels like to be in control of one's faculties.

According to a conservative view, we are most in control of ourselves when we empty our personalities of inappropriate "urges," of individual quirks, whims, drives, and compulsions that do not help us to "construct" a good, well-balanced self. But when we do manage this self-disciplinary task, and operate within the dictates of reason, virtue, conscience, and law, we find personal freedom. According to a contrary and less reverential view, we are most in control of ourselves when we are not disciplined, not controlled, not focused on commonsensical goals; when we pay close attention to our drives and urges, seize the day and do exactly as we please. Rocketing into ecstasy, we drink and dance and forget our limitations.

How can it be that we become ourselves by forgetting ourselves? Maybe the opposite is true, that we become ourselves by summoning our individuality, not burying it. The tension between finding and forgetting ourselves shapes this book. On the one hand, Ralph Waldo Emerson insists, "The one thing we seek with insatiable desire is to forget ourselves . . ."[2] On the other hand, introspection seems to lead to buried treasure. If we are to be true to ourselves, some will insist, we must turn inward. Here is how Boethius (b. 480) put it in *The Consolation of Philosophy:*

The man who searches deeply for the truth, and wishes to avoid being deceived by false leads, must turn the light of his inner vision upon himself. He must guide his soaring thoughts back again and teach his spirit that it possesses hidden among its own treasures whatever it seeks outside itself.[3]

Deep down inside us, then, lies a moral sensibility that squares with the wisdom of our neighbors. They are right, and we know it. Supposedly.

We rarely intend to harm ourselves, yet we can do so without meaning to. We can slip and fall (on the ice or on an object we didn't see) and suffer harm. We can ingest too many vitamins or spend too long in the tanning booth. Earlier generations did not know the harmful effects of cigarette smoking or did not fully grasp the difference safety belts could make in car accidents; as teenagers, our parents may have sneered at others who wore seat belts, avoided extended sun exposure, and declined cigarettes.

We might harm ourselves without meaning to in less obvious ways. We might allow emotions the dominant role in our decision-making: We might make choices after "listening to our heart" or feeling something "in our guts," for example. Or, through ignorance, we might lead our lives in ways we later regret (as Republicans, or fashion victims, or celibates). Giving in to our feelings and enjoying the surrender—this is raving, this is swooning. And this is arguably a manifestation of bad taste, of sentimentality, of emotional shallowness, of self-abuse.

Neighbors may quite reasonably interpret our apparent self-abuse as a cry for help. Concern for us can unleash their rescue fantasies, as concerned others try to save us from ourselves. Examples here run the gamut. In 1996, the *New York Times* profiled an evangelical Christian named Terry, who has devoted his life to "saving" drag queens or, as he calls them, eunuchs. Patrolling the West Side of Manhattan, Terry offers financial assistance and the support of his church congregation in Dallas. In turn, his recruits renounce their homosexuality and agree to join Terry's church fund-raising efforts (of course, some drag queens are heterosexual).[4]

Likewise, judges may act to stop us in our tracks. The American socialite Jocelyn Wildenstein divorced one of the world's wealthiest art collectors in 1999. She may hold the world record for undergoing cosmetic surgery, having even persuaded doctors to help her achieve the cat-like look she craved. In various photographs, Wildenstein looks as if she cannot blink—surgery has apparently compromised her facial muscles. In the divorce trial, the judge took the unusual step of stipulating that Wildenstein may not use any alimony payments (she was awarded two million dollars a year) for further cosmetic surgery.

What makes stepping out of line so compelling a subject is the disagreement it brings out between people as how best to use our freedom and how bad it is to do things to ourselves that we wouldn't dream of doing to others. This tension helps us appreciate the difficulty with which the State, our family, or a religious group will justify protecting us from ourselves.

We Reap What We Sow

Just as in autoimmune diseases our own immune system will attack our body, so in the course of settling into our skin do we sometimes orchestrate our own downfall. Our friends, fearful of the maxim "what goes around, comes around," may urge us to swear off gossip or speaking ill of others generally. The momentary pleasure will come back to haunt us, they warn, for those who live by the sword die by the sword. When people care about us, they naturally want to steer us away from pitfalls.

We as well want to avoid mistakes and so sometimes enlist the help of our friends. "Don't ever let me go crawling back to my ex-husband," a friend may insist. We might joke to our closest friend that we want him to quietly kill us if ever we wear a toupee, audition for a "reality" television show, or run for political office. We may quite legitimately fear harming ourselves by sliding into a way of thinking we presently consider abhorrent. The advance directives or "living wills" we may draw up with an attorney or upon admission to a hospital exist to prevent us from eventually assenting to treatment we think we should really avoid, from caving in to fear when we find ourselves at death's door (and also to prevent our relatives from making those same decisions for us once we've lost competence).

Moralists lie ready to blame us for the mistakes we make. Fair enough. What requires real effort to understand is how we can be blamed for biological functions, functions that allegedly harm us. Consider here nocturnal emissions and the mikvah. As I have noted, Augustine considered male masturbation—the spilling of seed—quite sinful. Curiously, Augustine holds men and boys responsible for nocturnal emissions, even though these occurrences are by their very nature involuntary. The event happens while a man sleeps and involves no conscious effort on his part. Similarly, menstruation is considered by Orthodox Jews something that makes a woman unclean, unfit to enter a temple. (Having sex with a menstruating woman makes a man unclean too.) An Orthodox Jewish woman must visit the mikvah, a ritual purification bath, before returning to the temple. And likewise, a scrupulous Catholic man or boy should confess his nocturnal emission(s) to a priest before receiving Holy Communion.

There don't seem to be any reasonable means to prevent the body from harming itself (if, in fact, it makes sense to put it that way: it may be that the censors are harming the person). How could a woman stop herself from menstruating? It is not impossible (for example, by following an extremely demanding athletic regimen or using the birth control pill strategically), but it is difficult. Similarly, some moralists—not just Catholic ones—have devised frankly surprising means by which men and boys can supposedly avoid or at least significantly decrease the likelihood of nocturnal emission. But here again, the strategy seeks to avoid something so natural that the sin or "harm" in question only seems more outlandish. Plenty of other thinkers have concluded that self-control ethics should begin with, rather than essentially ignore, the cravings of the body.

In the past, some devout Catholics have creatively combined physical and mental discipline. In his book *Introduction to the Devout Life* (1609), François de Sales recommends moderate the use of "the discipline," or whip, to the laity. Women as well as men were enjoined to flagellate themselves privately, to enhance communication with God. Gerard Manley Hopkins tortured himself spiritually, refusing to give in to baleful forces. Struggling with an invisible discipline, Hopkins wrote in "Carrion Comfort":

> Not, I'll not, carrion comfort, Despair, not feast on thee;
> Not untwist—slack they may be—these last strands of man
> In me or, most weary, cry *I can no more.* I can;
> Can something, hope, wish day come, not choose not to be.

Just as we gather our strength to fight infections or maladies, so can we summon the stamina to battle against forces that only we can feel. Catholic school boys learn to focus on the girl after whom they lust and imagine her as a skeleton (after all, we will all end up skeletons); the resulting picture should suffice to stave off sinful thoughts. Sometimes the fight against ourselves can become comical, showcasing the weakness of the will. In Italo Svevo's novel *Zeno's Conscience* (1920), the main character hilariously tries and fails to stop smoking. The one method he doesn't resort to is self-flagellation. While modern smokers eager to quit might cringe at the thought of whipping themselves, the discipline seemed to help monks and nuns in centuries past.

A life free of smoking and full of exercise points the way to longevity. To look good as we age, it seems only natural to take seriously the advice we find in self-help manuals and to listen to physicians. But getting carried away with exercise can lead to separate problems. Aging Hollywood actress Sharon Stone suffered a mild stroke after strenuously exercising. No pain, no gain, the forty-something star seemed to believe as she pushed herself. In a country obsessed with youth and beauty, more and more middle-aged American professionals are likely to follow the way of Sharon Stone, who refuses to go gently into old age. Doctors have since named the "Sharon Stone Syndrome" after her, convinced that they will need a label to describe other middle-aged enthusiasts in the near future.[5] Zeal for self-improvement can take you to the camp of those who cut off their nose to spite their face.

Ambition, closely related to zeal for self-improvement, can prompt egregious errors of judgment. Plagiarism is one of the best examples. In May 2003, *New York Times* reporter Jayson Blair joined Janet Cooke, formerly of the *Washington Post*, the *New Republic*'s Stephen Glass, the *Boston Globe*'s Patricia Smith, and Jay Forman of *Slate* as journalists who got caught embellishing, exaggerating, and outright lying in print. The practice spans disciplines, with academics and scientists inventing data, too. The year before Blair's downfall, Emory University history professor Michael A. Bellesiles resigned following an investigation of charges that he concocted evidence to support his book *Arming America;* American historian Doris Kearns Goodwin stepped down from a prestigious national board after her own plagiarism came to light; and Bell Labs fired researcher Jan Hendrik Schon when it discovered he made up scientific data and published it. Today, the Internet tempts many a college student to "cut and paste" paragraphs that will together constitute a term paper. If caught, students face severe penalties.

United States presidential candidate Gary Hart arguably showed even worse judgment than any skillful plagiarist when, in 1984, he challenged the press to catch him in adulterous conduct. Doing so turned out to be as challenging as shooting fish in a barrel. Some people seem to want to get caught. It is tempting but probably simplistic to interpret Hart's folly as a proverbial cry for help. He may be just another public figure who risks disgrace for private adventures or self-aggrandizement.

No More Nude Olympics

There is a difference between harming the self and not enhancing it (that is, not developing our talents). A tour of Europe or the Far East may enrich our education, but choosing not to go (because we don't have the required funds or time, or for whatever reason) doesn't necessarily *harm* the self (at least, it never did before 9/11). A missed opportunity is not an injury. We might in fact justify not going by referring to robberies, hijackings, and terrorist activities. The list of ways in which we can improve and enhance ourselves keeps on expanding. Advertisements for face lifts, breast reductions, and penile enlargements greet us regularly in magazines and newspapers; they promise more satisfying interactions with others and greater self-esteem. Yet again, efforts to improve and enhance ourselves may lead to harm. Face lifts can fail, as can penile enlargement procedures. Women with faulty silicone breast implants have brought lawsuits against their doctors; surely it's just a matter of time before men follow suit. You could say that the streets are paved with bills for bad nose jobs, tummy tucks, hormone replacement therapy regimens, hair replacement therapy programs, and on and on.

Friends don't let friends drive drunk, even in remote areas where a car crash would only involve our friend. Friends don't let friends succumb to bad influences either. That's what friends are for, after all.

Perhaps that's what civilization is for as well. Sometimes laws are enacted in order to prevent us from hurting ourselves. Prisoners taken into custody will be searched for potential weapons—out of a fear that they will try to harm themselves in solitary confinement. Patients admitted into psychiatric wards will be guarded and/or sedated in order to prevent the same end. We do not allow children to drive (even though they might be able to help us out by doing so) out of a fear that they will harm themselves (and, quite possibly, others). Surely there are many other examples. Consider a colorful collegiate one. Princeton University banned what came to be known as the "Nude Olympics" and adopted the following policy:

> For a number of years undergraduates, predominantly members of the sophomore class, have gathered as a group in Holder Courtyard on the night of the first snowfall, virtually naked, and in an environment that includes student alcohol abuse, underage drinking, lack of concern for the welfare of fellow students, and *risk of harm to themselves,* other people, and property. This gathering has come to be known as the "nude olympics." The Committee on the Nude Olympics recommends to President Shapiro and the Board of Trustees that the University ban the nude olympics. In addition, the Committee recommends that the undergraduate student body be advised that they may not attempt to organize or engage in any activity that is perceived to perpetuate gatherings or events that contain or encourage some or all of the behaviors that, as noted above, have been associated with past nude olympics. These prohibitions should apply to the campus, as well as public and private property in the surrounding communities [my italics].[6]

Across the country, professors regularly grumble about boring committee assignments. Princeton University professors likely regret the unlikelihood of ever again serving so interesting a cause as the Committee on the Nude Olympics. Be that as it may, University officials may well have been justified in spoiling the youthful folly of their students.

In the spring of 2001, the chief academic officer of the University of Michigan followed suit. She urged her faculty and administrators to discourage students from taking part in the "Naked Mile." In a letter that appeared in the *University Record* on April 9, 2001, she explained:

> Most of you are aware of the upcoming campus tradition known as the Naked Mile. I am writing this letter to keep you informed of our growing concerns about this event, which has evolved into a dangerous experience for our students.
>
> The run, which began in 1986, has grown out of control in recent years. Thousands of spectators gather, many of them with the intent of videotaping the participants or grabbing at runners as they traverse what quickly becomes a narrow gauntlet. Many runners who were motivated by the enthusiasm of the moment, further fueled by alcohol, later expressed regret at having participated.
>
> Participants are subjecting themselves to potential assault, arrest and serious physical harm; and there is the very real likelihood that the consequences of their actions will come back to haunt students far into the future. Arrests for alcohol violations and indecent exposure are a matter of public record and may affect their career prospects. In addition, videotapes and photographs of the student participants appear widely on the Internet and may prove to be of considerable embarrassment to them down the road.[7]

Michigan's stance proved softer than Princeton's, but both schools moved to prevent students from doing what they wanted. Not so long ago, *Playboy* magazine featured photographic layouts with names like "Women of the Ivy League" and "Women of the Big 10." It would be interesting to poll well-educated pin-ups of two decades ago and inquire about regret. Veterans of the Nude Olympics and the Naked Mile might surprise us too. They might smile when asked.

These examples involve universities acting to remove people from occasions in which they might harm themselves. The prescription of drugs such as Prozac to diminish the likelihood that a depressed person will harm him or herself no doubt elicits broader public concern. Psychiatrists are legally compelled to prescribe psychotropic drugs when they believe a patient's life is in danger. And, as I've said, prison officials are expected to remove sharp objects and rope from the confines of any inmate suspected of harboring a death wish.

You may wonder why we continue to force people who do not want to live to stay alive. In a prison or in a hospital, employees who see suicidal people professionally are bound by law, certainly. But beyond the public sphere? Both the State and religious authorities, like friends and family members, reason that emotional chaos prompts suicidal people to want to kill themselves. Once we tame the chaos, those people will surely want to go on living. The sufferers will thank us for having protected him from them from themselves. Or so the reasoning has gone for centuries.

It will surprise no one that popular opinion changes from era to era with regard to how far we may go in preventing others from harming themselves, or even what constitutes harm. Roughly one out of every ten Americans, for example, has taken Prozac, Zoloft, or Paxil, or a similar antidepressant. Some voices from the medical sphere allege that these celebrated drugs actually do harm us. Dr. Joseph Glenmullen, a psychiatrist at Harvard University Health Services, depicts an "antidepressant mania" in *Prozac Backlash*, a trend he considers not only dangerous but also reckless.[8] He alerts us to the severe side effects of drugs, which include uncontrollable facial and body tics and perhaps even permanent brain damage. He reports that roughly fifty percent of patients experience debilitating withdrawal symptoms from them, and about sixty percent end up with sexual problems of some sort. Further, Prozac may make a small number of people homi-cidal or sui-cidal, or both. (Critics will not doubt take issue with Glenmullen's data and insist that the most alarming side effects, like tics and Parkinsonism, are rare.)

* * *

THERE IS A DIFFERENCE BETWEEN SCIENCE GETTING IT right and a culture shifting beneath our feet. As to the second, think of nudity again. In *The Civilizing Process* Norbert Elias describes the streets of northern and middle Europe around the time of the Renaissance:

> It seems to have been common practice, at least in the towns, to undress at home before going to the bathhouse. "How often," says an observer, "the father, wearing nothing but his breeches, with his naked wife and children, runs through the streets from his house to the baths.... How many times have I seen girls of ten, twelve, fourteen, sixteen, and eighteen years entirely naked except for a short smock, often torn, and a ragged bathing gown at front and back? With this open at the feet and with their hands held decorously behind them, running from their houses through the long streets at midday to the baths. How many completely naked boys of ten, twelve, fourteen, and sixteen run beside them...."[9]

Shocking. This indulgent attitude toward public nudity differs markedly from the Nude Olympics. How so? No alcohol is involved in the Elias example, nor photography. Presumably it is not snowing. But Princeton officials wouldn't smile on a Nude Olympics held in the late spring, even if alcohol could effectively be eliminated from the festivities. Civil laws prohibit indecent exposure. Princeton University administrators worry about eventual student regret.

Interestingly, Wesleyan University officials expressed a sense of futility in a front-page *New York Times* article on a "naked dorm" there.[10] Students in one particular dormitory were permitted to wander freely about the building and outside lawn while naked. Wesleyan administrators explained that the university did not specifically ban nudity, out of fear that the prohibition would only encourage nudity.

Paternalism blends into *noblesse oblige,* the idea that social superiors need to look out for social inferiors. Adults need to watch over children, just as the socially privileged owe a helping hand to the socially underprivileged. Curiously, people with money apparently thought of working for a living (which they did not have to do) as only part of the reason why the lower classes should seek employment. The other and arguably more important reason was to keep them out of trouble ("Idle hands are the devil's workshop"). We find this logic in a passage from the early twentieth-century (and, incidentally, wealthy) philosopher Bertrand Russell in 1932:

> The idea that the poor should have leisure has always been shocking to the rich. In England, in the early nineteenth century, fifteen hours was the ordinary day's work for a man; children sometimes did as much, and very commonly did twelve hours a day. When meddlesome busybodies suggested that perhaps these hours were rather long, they were told that work kept adults from drink and children from mischief.[11]

Russell looked forward to a future in which a full day's work would span four hours. In the increasingly demanding and frenetic world of corporate dominance (and, to be fair, of inordinate greed and enthusiastic materialistic consumption), precisely the opposite has happened.

Law and morality work in concert to prevent public nudity, such that we have more to worry about than the malicious gossip of neighbors and colleagues. Obscenity provides an excellent example of how others protect us from ourselves, while they protect themselves at the same time. The United States Supreme Court established a standard of what is harmful to adults in 1973, five years after it had articulated the threshold of what is harmful to minors. According to the 1973 case *Miller v. California,* obscenity must be "patently offensive" and appeal to the "prurient interest"; "community standards" dictate the application of these criteria, which means that a book or television show may pass muster in Manhattan but not in Omaha; and the work must lack "serious legal, artistic, political, or scientific value." In 1973, the Court lowered the obscenity threshold slightly; in 1968, the Court had marshaled the same criteria in *Ginsberg v. New York* to establish obscenity standards for children. The difference between the two rulings comes down to the stringency with which the criteria are applied. In both cases, the Court seemed to affirm the difficulty of measuring what's bad for us.

Styles of Harm to the Self

The discrete ways in which we can harm ourselves fall roughly into four categories:

· *Physically.* Common sense and the medical world tell us that when we destroy, diminish, or pollute our bodies, we make life harder. We need a healthy body to weather life's storms. Tobacco smoke, excessive alcohol intake, and a high-fat diet will shorten our life span and increase the chance that we will suffer poor health. Beyond that, more immediate worries loom. If we do not make ourselves as beautiful as possible, we will not get invited to many parties, people will be less likely to talk to us when we do, and we may be passed over for promotions at work.

Earlier I discussed the asphyxiation of teenage boys engaged in intense masturbatory exercises. But we should not discount the widespread dangers teenagers regularly encounter in apparently healthy sports activities. For many teens, extreme sports represent the essence of "cool" and the cutting edge. Not surprisingly, severe injuries have resulted from activities with skis, snowboards, surfboards, kayaks, scooters, skateboards, bikes, motorcycles, rollerblades, luges, toboggans, not to mention mountaineering.

· *Spiritually.* For believers, when we disobey God's law we make it less likely that we will reach heaven or its equivalent. This exigency figures into Judaism, Christianity, and Islam, and is significant to all organized religions and probably to many unorganized ones as well. But even people who feel distant from organized religion will recognize that we must maintain hope in something better; despair strangles the inner life.

· *Socially.* There is no end to the ways we can damage our social standing. As First Lady of the United States, Nancy Reagan harmed her reputation by apparently relying on a psychic for guidance. She nearly alienated the Christian Right, a force that helped her husband reach the White House.

If we do not cultivate cordial relationships with those around us, we receive less sympathy when we suffer. It always used to be that the world expected us to keep a "stiff upper lip" in the face of personal hardship; tell-all talk shows on television have begun to change this. The best remedy for social gaffes now seems to be tearful, public confessions (although United States Senator Trent Lott failed to turn the tide with his). Compassion comes flooding in, if you've done your homework.

Some kids will deliberately avoid achieving high grades in school in an effort to appear cool to their peers. By hurting their chances to get into college, these kids may be shooting themselves in the foot.

We especially risk ourselves in friendship and romantic liaisons (as many a TV soap opera or sitcom tells us—think of *Seinfeld, Friends,* or *Sex and the City*). The media has driven home these lessons. One need only think of the friendship between Monica Lewinsky and Linda Tripp (the latter secretly tape recorded conversations and used the tapes against her friend in order to bring down President Clinton) or the adulterous love affair between Princess Diana and James Hewitt (the latter publicly auctioned off love letters written to him by the Duchess of Wales) to see that we risk harming ourselves by confiding in others. Kiss-and-tell books such as *No Lifeguard on Duty*, by a former supermodel, gossip about the bedroom prowess or ineptitude of various leading men in Hollywood.[12] Even casual flings among mere mortals can backfire. In 2003, a Duke graduate named Tucker Max published in an online diary (also known as a "blog") details of his lurid affair with Miss Vermont 1999. First Amendment rights protected Mr. Max, who claimed that this woman who publicly advocates abstinence from sex and alcohol privately breaks her own vows.[13] We trust others at our own risk.

· *Emotionally*. Emotional damage that we can bring to ourselves through self-harm is tremendous. Sometimes it can be passing, sometimes permanent. Take, for instance, "regret" for not having pursued some goal in life we thought we wanted (a profession, a skill, a partner, etc.) Maybe we refused to keep up with those cello lessons when we were young enough to learn. Or maybe we lost custody of our kids because we were drinking too much. Maybe we didn't make peace with our mother right before her death.

A world of things to regret in life can harm us. We feel convinced that life would have been better had we married someone else, gone to a different university, pursued a different profession.... In most cases, we really can't know whether we are right, but on some level, it doesn't matter a great deal. The point is that we believe we have damaged our lives, ourselves in some way—either our sense of happiness, or of self-respect or self-worth, or of goodness as a human being.

Of course, these four categories sometimes overlap. Various examples illuminate these intersections. According to an old stereotype, gay men resort to promiscuity in order to escape a hostile world. Despite the threat of disease, they ecstatically pursue self-abandon through anonymous sex. In so doing, they harm themselves physically, socially and emotionally—and even spiritually according to those who believe in God.

It can't be said today that religion lurks behind most Western legal definitions of immoral behavior, or that belief in God dictates whether we can harm the self and what those harms might be. But religion can certainly creep into prevailing cultural notions of right and wrong. In a 1965 essay entitled "The Enforcement of Morals," an English philosopher named Patrick Devlin argued that a society should make illegal any act found disgusting to 51 percent of its population.[14] Clearly, if a society were largely religious in some specific sense and Devlin's untenable rule were instituted, the criminal law would largely overlap with religious sensibilities. Such odd possibilities aside, it is perhaps in the question of what we may or may not do to ourselves that vestiges of a more God-oriented culture most obviously manifest themselves.

The Shame of It

Kind-hearted people put ropes around us, then, for a legitimate reason. They want to save us from regret—and shame as well.

Why is it that some of us regularly feel shame, while others rarely do? The world may blame me for doing something it considers harmful to myself, and I may shrug off the blame. The world may blame you for supposedly harming yourself in some way, and you may burn with shame. The difference between us may come down to moral imagination: Some people lack the mental capacity to project the consequences of acts into the future, or to internalize the very real concerns of others. What interests me here are people who accept the judgment of others that they have harmed themselves in some way and then regret their act.

The mistakes we make on our own deserve special attention. Sophocles and Schopenhauer both came to the conclusion that the greatest suffering is that which we bring upon ourselves. I agree. Suffering is somehow easier to bear if we can blame it on someone else. So, with good reason, parents, teachers, and spiritual and financial advisors strive to prevent us from hurting ourselves.

One of the most effective ways others prevent us from committing what they take to be self-destructive acts is to attach shame and guilt to those acts or attitudes. We may see such acts or attitudes as simple carelessness or fleeting respites from boredom or unhappy situations—perhaps even our natural rights as citizens in a democracy. Others, however, may differ. They may shame us into another perspective.

It must be true that we get ourselves into more trouble by harming others than we do by harming ourselves. Robbing, assaulting, or cheating others will outrage our neighbors. But we will nonetheless suffer plenty of shame if they catch us neglecting our honor.

What is particularly interesting about shame is its aura of having exposed an irreversible truth. At long last, others have found us out. They have seen our true colors. They've found the weak spot, the hidden thing, the Achilles heel. What is revealed in shame is not an answer, a solution, or a key to self-understanding: not why we do what we do. What is illuminated is the abiding mystery of something that has been discovered which should have remained hidden: What we do is what we are. In shame we feel more keenly than ever what others think of us: We see ourselves as others see us, colored by our indiscretion or need or laxnesss or looseness. Tabloid headlines.

How hard it can be to live within a community we don't feel a part of. It is enough to note that we use shame to keep people in line. If shamelessness is on the rise, as so many social commentators in America have insisted since the 1960s countercultural revolution, then others are losing ground in their power to manipulate our behavior. However, shame will surely never recede entirely from our lives, which means we will always have an incentive to hide from others. Yet, hiding from others, in any form, is frequently risky. As long as others hold us accountable for our actions and characters, they will find ways of discovering what we have hidden. As a way of persuading us to live as they see fit, they will urge self-control on us.

Surrender Never

A focus on our private freedom and our unspoken hopes reveals dizzying layers of complexity. A fear of success cripples some talented people; they may take to sabotaging their own chances of promotion at work or acclaim in the media. Getting what we want sometimes disappoints us, it turns out, or scares us. Getting married, promoted at work, licensed to drive race cars, or loaded on a Friday night may leave us feeling empty and more dejected than the day before. Moving into what we see as our true selves might be as simple as swearing off what's bad for us. And yet, many passionate souls will heed the call of the wild and begin a titillating dance with what's bad for us.

When others protect us from ourselves, they tell us something about themselves. If we are charitably disposed, we will conclude that they care for us and seek to promote what they consider our best interests (even though we may disagree). We may, however, suspect that they are acting selfishly: They themselves do not want to live in a world in which tattooed people with nose rings and eyelid piercings teach their children or serve them food in restaurants. And so they will make it hard for us to tattoo or pierce ourselves. If they fail to make something we do outright illegal, they will wave us off, accusing us of having flown off the rails.

By now, the strong moral support on which they can draw should be clear. I have held up two different philosophers as roughly representative of the struggle between what we may wish to do with or to ourselves and what others will permit. John Stuart Mill seeks to free us from the tyranny of others, whereas Immanuel Kant strives to help us see our duty to humanity through the exercise of self-control. Kant does not see himself enslaving us to a rigid moral code, but teaching us to appreciate its wondrous beauty. For Kant, we obey the law because we love it.

Does his abiding sternness mean that Kant fails to recognize the shortcomings of human beings? Not at all. He insists that the moral law must rigorously demand "the highest perfection of social morality." It must not, he insists, indulge man and make allowance for his limited capacity. The standard of moral excellence must be "exact, invariable and absolute," despite our human weaknesses. Self-control catapults us over those weaknesses.

part two

Self-Control

chapter five

Self-Control

IN 1998, TELEVISION PERSONALITY SUSAN ESTRICH PUB-
lished a diet book. A woman of many achievements, Estrich
earned tenure at the Harvard Law School after having distin-
guished herself as a student, when she became the first woman
ever to head the *Harvard Law Review*. Estrich went on to become the first woman ever to manage a presidential campaign
(Walter Mondale's, in 1980). In her diet book, Estrich claimed
that the life achievement of which she was most proud was
moving from a dress size of 12 to 6. Conquering the world
meant less to her than conquering her weight gains.

Are we so different? Probably not. On some level many of
us already know that the biggest obstacle to worldly success
or spiritual redemption is ourselves. We are bad for us. According to her account, Estrich lost control of herself and,
against her better judgment, overate. She was herself to blame
for her biggest problem, and so the weakness of will that facil-
itated overeating must be bad.

When it comes to self-control, what people want more
than anything is instruction on how to get more of it. Setting
two alarm clocks, or setting the clock ten minutes fast, or setting the scale ten pounds heavier, we devise ingenious ways
to trick ourselves into discipline. Self-control stands as one of
the central mysteries of human experience. Friends around
the world get together and sooner or later ponder where self-
control comes from.

The Muscle Within

Self-control emanates from within us, which is about all that can be said about the source. With the possible exception of psychiatrists, no one can give it to us. The more we exercise the muscle, the stronger it becomes. Use it or lose it.

Self-control differs from control. Politicians and celebrities, for example, sacrifice an enormous amount of privacy in order to enjoy the careers they do. Doctors, salesmen, and an increasingly broad spectrum of workers now carry with them cell telephones and Palm Pilots in order to allow clients and colleagues to contact them at any hour of the day or night. In addition, they often have a secretary, a beeper, voice mail, and a telefax machine at home. What do you do if you just want to be alone? Modern professionals, like politicians and celebrities, may not have much control over silence, but they may still have plenty of self-control. On another level, the same difficulty plays itself out in the family: The decision to have children, for all but the very wealthy, amounts to a sacrifice of control over much of one's life.

Self-control regularly looms over dramas (the real and the fictional). Self-control is sexy, but then so is losing it. Losing self-control can sometimes scare others, other times seduce them.

Many of our best-known stories center on the problem of too much or too little self-control. Classical literature is steeped in tragedies of madness, revenge, folly, shame, guilt, and disgrace. In Virgil's *Aeneid,* for example, Dido loses self-control when her Trojan lover Aeneas abandons her. Knowing where and when his ship will pass the shore, she quickly constructs a tall pyre, the flames from which everyone on board will surely see. At the crucial moment, she curses Aeneas and stabs herself next to the pyre, where she had all along intended for her funeral rites to be held. Writers have frequently deployed the absence, or excess, of self-control as a plot device.

Cervantes's *Don Quixote,* often referred to as the first modern novel, uses the theme of illusion and lack of self-control as the basis of the entire work. The mad, dreamy protagonist, confusing storybook tales with real life, flouts social expectations and refuses to police himself in the way others require. Many readers will be left wondering whether Don Quixote is the crazy one, or whether we are crazy to live by the rules he defies. Self-control comes off as something steely and cold in this work, just as it does in Madame de Lafayette's *Princess of Clèves,* a seminal work in French literature. The beautiful and virtuous princess in this late seventeenth-century novel gradually realizes that she does not love her husband. She yearns for M. de Nemours, whom she sees daily at the court of the king, but she disguises her affection. When he takes a sudden fall one day, the zeal with which she rushes to his side betrays her. But when her husband conveniently dies, she refuses to accept Nemours's earnest proposal of marriage, out of fear that his love for her might one day fade, as it had for other women. She refuses him in the name of her faithful, now dead husband. Mustering self-control so thorough that it seems inhuman, she takes the veil and, with it, her leave from society. Her life, we are told at the end of the novel, was not a long one, but noted for its inimitable (unenviable?) goodness.

Nineteenth- and twentieth-century novels are filled with characters who either overuse or underuse their self-control. Emma Bovary has affairs and, finally, takes arsenic. Anna Karenina also has an affair and, finally, jumps in front of a train. Bill Sikes murders Nancy. The Invisible Man runs rampant, Raskolnikov plays cat-and-mouse badly with the police, Captain Ahab leads his ship to destruction for the sake of the White Whale, and Sherlock Holmes keeps order in place only with the help of drugs.

Of the myriad films, plays, and works of literature that employ self-control as a crucial plot device, few can exceed in beauty Franz Kafka's poignant short story "The Hunger

Artist." Kafka conveys the sadness of a man whose talent at self-control has ceased to interest the world. The hunger artist was a sideshow at the circus; crowds gawked at him in his cage and marveled at the daily announcement of how long he had gone without eating. The hunger artist made a living out of publicly overcoming human desire; then, after years of popularity, he came to see himself dying not of malnutrition, but neglect. Even as circus-goers increasingly passed his cage with indifference, the hunger artist steeled up his resolve. Self-control made him superhuman.

The ugly underside of self-control finds masterful expression in Ian McEwan's novel *Atonement*.[1] A precocious thirteen-year-old with an insatiable appetite for attention and drama buzzes around adults who fail to take her seriously enough. A dreamer, "Briony was lost to her fantasies." She resolves to become a writer in order to win the admiration of both her family and the world. "What she wanted was to be lost to the unfolding of an irresistible idea." Sensing the possibility of raw power, she identifies a young man as the rapist wanted by local police and basks in the gratitude of all but her older sister Cecilia, who knows Briony could not have seen the actual rapist in the pitch dark, as she had claimed. Cecilia, in love with the accused, had been with him. Cecilia bitterly resents Briony's resolve, the naive, cold control she exhibits over other people's futures. Briony thrills to the sense that, at last, she is being taken seriously: "And though it horrified her, it was another entry, a moment of coming into being, another first: to be hated by an adult. Children hated generously, capriciously. It hardly mattered. But to be the object of adult hatred was an initiation into a solemn new world. It was promotion.... Briony felt vindicated by the reaction of the adults, who she thought took her more seriously for denying her lack of self-control. After a night of police interrogation, Briony found her way to bed just as the sun rose." Missing the spotlight she had enjoyed for hours, she began to cry: "She turned her face into the pillow and let her tears drain into it, and felt that yet more was lost when there was no witness to her sorrow." Briony grows up only to spend her adulthood regretting the unspeakable damage she did to the young man, who served time in prison then died a soldier in World War II, and to the woman who never stopped loving him—her sister, Cecilia, who also died in the war.

Briony never cracked throughout the trial; the steely resolve of a thirteen-year-old to pretend she knew what she didn't comes across as monstrous. Any child with a heart would have fallen apart and confessed to doubt. Self-control haunts Briony until she dies. What most of us end up regretting is the loss of self-control, which only increases the power of McEwan's novel.

In real life, the consequences of failing to maintain self-control can be political: An entire nation might decline and fall. Think of the Russians' current problem controlling the level of alcohol consumption, especially among men, and the difficulties alcoholism brings to the beleaguered "new" Russia. Think, too, of the cruelty of the breakup of Yugoslavia, where ethnic hatreds replaced civil entente. Think of the Chinese and opium addiction. We can tell that a nation's value system has suffered erosion when we detect a lack of self-control in its populace at large. According to Zbigniew Brzezinski:

> Our ability to understand the wider ramifications of the present—not to speak of the future—is impeded by the massive collapse, especially in the advanced parts of the world, of almost all established values. Totalitarian doctrines have been discredited—and that is to be applauded. But the role of religion in defining moral standards has also declined while an ethos of consumerism masquerades as a substitute for *ethical standards.* Humanity's capacity to control itself and its environment has been expanding exponentially and our material expectations even more so. At the same time, our social criteria of moral discernment and of self-control have become increasingly vague.[2]

Lack of self-control among individuals will diminish the nation as a whole, Brzezinski believes. A virtue, self-control can be cultivated. When we do not find it in others, they are to blame.

Public versus private. This Enlightenment view of civic life contrasts with the older, more private one of falling in love. The ancient Greeks thought of love as a fatality of sorts. When Cupid hit you with his arrow, you were to be pitied. You took leave of reason. Your friends surrounded you and lamented your ill fortune. You lost your self-control. Against the familiar picture of love as irrational, a surrender to darkly invisible forces, though, we should recognize rival depictions. A compelling—one could say neo-Enlightenment—depiction of love as measured and reflective surfaces in the 1988 Wim Wenders film *Der Himmel über Berlin* (translated into English as *The Wings of Desire;* Hollywood remade this film in 1998 as *City of Angels*). In this evocative film, two angels land on Earth as punishment for wrongdoing. Their corner of Earth happens to be Berlin, Wenders's own city. The two angels yearn to experience mortal pleasures, particularly love. Damiel, one of the angels, falls in love with a lonely but beautiful trapeze artist, who recognizes him as THE ONE the instant she seems him. Marion, the trapeze artist, poetically equates falling in love with getting serious about life, that is, self-control.[3] If we try to see love from the perspectives of ancient Greeks *and* Enlightenment thinkers, we may come to the conclusion that in love we curiously seek both to extinguish and expand ourselves (this is the theme of much Romantic poetry), in order to regulate our inner life.

Self-control: For Us or Them?

Self-control provides what we need in order to behave well even when others don't, or even when no one can see us. The key to happiness in life lies in self-control, in curbing our desire to do what's bad for us. Why do we say no to ourselves when we want to say yes? For two different reasons: us and them.

Think of a similar question: Why do Mercedes drivers choose a car that represents elegance? Are they trying to impress others, or do they simply, genuinely enjoy the luxury of a Mercedes? Skeptics may roll their eyes, but I think most of us will agree that it is at least possible that Mercedes owners make their decisions based on themselves, not us. While they sit behind the wheel, they slip into an appealing vision of themselves. They may or may not care about our admiration.

Why do we behave? Are we trying to please others or live up to a personal goal? I think good behavior actually stems from selfish desires at least as often as it does from a wish to meet the expectations of others. Think of marriage: I may remain faithful to my spouse not so much because I feel I have to, but because I want to be the kind of person who doesn't cheat. I do it for myself. Years into my marriage, I may discover that my spouse has cheated on me. I may feel devastated, but I don't feel I've wasted my fidelity. All along, I was being the kind of person I wanted to be. I don't resent my spouse for having taken something from me. If ever I enter another relationship, I can say truthfully that I was always faithful to a person who ultimately cheated on me. I couldn't control my spouse's behavior, but I could control mine. And did.

For the most part, we can decide for ourselves what sort of spouse to be. And depending on the financial sacrifices we are willing to make, we can decide what kind of car to drive. We can't always decide what's good for us, though. For we are born into little worlds which have already determined what's bad for us.

Just Do It

Judeo-Christian tradition parts with ancient Greek tradition over the question of self-control. Socrates insisted that to know the good is to do the good, which meant that misdeeds came down to *ignorance*. Bad people hadn't quite gotten it yet, that's all. Once we teach them what is right, they will surely obey, just as we do. According to many religious thinkers, though, misdeeds come down to *poor self-control*. Once Adam and Eve spoiled things for the rest of us, knowing the right thing to do simply wasn't enough. You had to muster the discipline to follow through on your knowledge. When you fail, you deserve blame because your base instincts or laziness got the better of you. Sin comes down to a lack of self-control. Redemption arises from the possibility that we can overcome the parts of ourselves we wish away.

Whether in love or war, Aristotle worried more about young men than about anyone else. "Young men have strong passions, and tend to gratify them indiscriminately. Of the bodily desires, it is the sexual by which they are most swayed and in which they show absence of self-control" (*Rhetoric*, Book II, chapter 11), he warned. "They are changeable and fickle in their desires, which are violent while they last, but quickly over: Their impulses are keen but not deep-rooted, and are like sick people's attacks of hunger and thirst. They are hot-tempered and quick-tempered, and apt to give way to their anger...."

Following Aristotle, subsequent moralists argued that (male) self-control could be taught through the body. In adolescence, young men had to be taught to respect their bodies. "You cannot give way to any appetite, without feeling instant and constant degradation," warned a New England minister, John Todd, in a manual printed and reprinted in the nineteenth century, *The Young Man: Hints Addressed to the Young Men of the United States*. "Conscience can be deadened and murdered in no way so readily as by such indulgence."[4] The ambitious young man must not give in to selfish, "natural" desires. He must control not only his sexual drive but also his taste for strong drink and rich, spicy food. In most medical theories of the era, beginning with Benjamin Rush in the late eighteenth century and continuing through Sylvester Graham's interpretations in the 1830s, these three appetites had a reciprocal influence on one another. Highly spiced foods, too much meat, certain kinds of shellfish, and all forms of alcohol could inflame the system and stir up the embers of lust. Indulging in such victuals was both sign and cause of weakening discipline. In addition to suggesting that these stimulants be avoided, the concept of self-regulation called for a young man not to be lazy and not to squander his time and energy on such useless activities as light reading and frivolous conversation. The young Victorian developed and sharpened character by mastering in all areas of life his too-human propensity for the easy path and immediate gratification.

Throughout human history, sexual regulation has seemed to demand the regulation of other impulses. Although modern Western parents may lose no sleep over thoughts of a masturbating son in the house, sexual activity likely remains the appetite they most wish to regulate. Controlling his insistent carnality is a young man's triumphant proof of willpower. After winning the battle with lust, the growing youth may go on to master other battles as well—drink, drugs, wild driving, rudeness, laziness, and so on.

In the New Testament, St. Paul voices similar worries. He urges self-control to those without the superhuman strength of will necessary to swear off sex permanently. He exhorts: "To the unmarried and the widows I say that it is well for them to remain single as I do. But if they cannot exercise self-control, they should marry. For it is better to marry than to be aflame with passion" (1 Corinthians 7:8–9). This advice would make little sense without a corresponding belief that we are in some important sense slaves to our passions. If you cannot stop having sex, take a wife. At least you'll only be having sex with one person (one woman, that is).

For many people, lust poses an even greater challenge to self-control than does greed. (For one, sex is usually cheap and easily obtained. Material wealth is not.) A new medical treatment for a new disease provides a useful occasion for appreciating the power of lust over mere mortals. The American essayist Andrew Sullivan, who suffers from HIV infection, has spoken openly of his condition and the salubrious effect of testosterone injections. In the *New York Times Magazine*, he revealed that one of the surprising consequences of these injections was the sharp increase in his sex drive. These periodic yet regular increases (he injected himself biweekly) caused him to reflect on lust and the pattern his libido had established long before being diagnosed with a deadly disease. Sullivan mused:

> The odd thing is that, however much experience I have with it, this lust peak still takes me unawares. It is not like feeling hungry, a feeling you recognize and satiate. It creeps up on you.... You realize more acutely than before that lust is a chemical. It comes; it goes. It waxes; it wanes. You are not helpless in front of it, but you are certainly not fully in control.[5]

The urge to help others achieve self-control may lead to physical intervention. The lines blur. Contemporary Americans have criticized Muslim and other traditional African cultures for performing the clitoridectomy. This procedure is usually performed on young girls in hopes that they will grow up to be chaste, compliant, faithful wives. In fact, many of them will experience lifelong gynecological problems, some very serious and painful. In the late nineteenth century, some American women came to perceive passion as dangerous enough to demand a cliterodectomy for themselves. The procedure attained some popularity from the 1870s through 1900. The last clitoridectomy performed in the United States occurred as recently as 1948, as a "cure" for the habit of masturbation in a five-year-old girl. Although never accepted in Europe and rejected by many American doctors, clitoridectomies appealed to some as the ultimate weapon against female pathological passion.[6] Today, human rights observers strive to win worldwide condemnation of this cruel practice.

We turn to self-control to achieve clarity of mind. Where do our thoughts come from? Why do some people have intellectually sophisticated thoughts when others, in the same classroom day after day, can think only of lunch? To what extent can we claim credit for our brilliant thoughts and ideas? Presence of mind would seem to come down to luck, which is not to say that we can't work to enhance our powers. In any event, we are rarely blamed for our mental dullness, but we may be led to feel guilty for lustful or violent images that pop into our heads. St. Teresa of Avila both feared and wondered at her thoughts:

> It sometimes happens that the intellect and the soul are so troubled and distracted that they couldn't put together a coherent sentence, and yet the soul finds itself being served up impressive speeches that it couldn't concoct by itself, even if it were completely recollected—and at the first word, as I said the soul is thoroughly transformed. If it is in a rapture, especially, and if its faculties are suspended, how can it possibly understand things that have never occurred to it before? How can those things come to it at a time when the memory is hardly functioning, and the imagination is more or less stunned?[7]

Centuries later, the Austrian philosopher Ludwig Wittgenstein (d. 1951) would puzzle over how our minds can understand sentences they have never heard before. He never considered the devil as an explanation, as St. Teresa had.

Self-control has dictated gender expectations. Take anger, for example. A woman who expresses her anger and strikes out at another has failed to manage her emotions effectively; she's being a "harridan," "hysterical," or "menopausal." A man who openly displays his anger inspires confidence: He knows how to stick up for himself, for his family, and perhaps for us. We are more likely to vote for him or support him when he runs into one of life's obstacles; he gets things done. Not so for the angry woman: we call her "pushy" or a "bitch" and castigate her. Of course, there is a difference between displaying anger and losing control. The man whose anger goes over the top does not win our confidence; he's "crazy." The point is that, as difficult as it may be for us to control ourselves, others often fail to understand. Exasperated, they counsel us, "Just do it."

Will They Respect Us in the Morning?

How curious, this idea that we must battle against ourselves. Pagan, Jewish, and Christian thinkers (among others) have concurred that we can indeed be our own worst enemies. As we walk through life, the threat from without may only slightly exceed the threat from within. Self-control, both emotional and physical, is as necessary to getting ahead in business as it is to getting to heaven.

Modern compassion differs from erstwhile sympathy. Whereas we used to pity people because they could not resist temptation, we now pity them because they cannot resist themselves. Unwanted thoughts, desires, and impulses swell up within us and express themselves through our transgressions. Our modern view of individuals imprisoned by chemical imbalances in the brain compels us to urge therapy on many wrongdoers, not censure them (I'll turn to this idea in chapter seven). We may find that we ourselves must resort to self-control to avoid blaming people for their own faults.

Many op-ed pieces, essays, and books since the 1960s have sought to alarm us into acknowledging an epidemic: People can't control themselves anymore. Daniel Bell argued in an influential book from 1976, *The Cultural Contradictions of Capitalism,* that capitalism rests on a paradox: The worker has to be self-disciplined enough to show up for work every day on time, but he or she has to want "the good life" enough to want to work hard, in order to earn the money needed to remain the consumer he or she wants to be. Like Max Weber before him, Bell believed the Protestant work ethic had married these two impulses harmoniously. Bell, however, pointed to evidence around him that self-restraint and self-discipline were disappearing. According to Bell, the widespread enthusiasm for self-knowledge and self-exploration fanned the flames of consumerism. Cultural preoccupation was shifting from a focus on how to work and achieve to a focus on how to spend and enjoy. It seemed plausible to him to think that capitalism would unleash cultural forces that would end up destroying it.

Can we carry self-control or self-discipline too far? Perhaps not, if we're being spied on. The modern West seems to be moving ever closer to the society envisaged by George Orwell in *1984*. Big Brother keeps getting better at watching us, and the circumstances under which people interact with one another, particularly e-mail, seem to facilitate surveillance. Even after we delete e-messages we have written or received, they can be retrieved by savvy technicians. Every Web site we visit on the Internet leaves a mark (or "cookie") on our computers as well. When White House intern Monica Lewinsky was subpoenaed by Kenneth Starr, he took the dramatic step of removing the hard drive from her home computer. He also legally compelled Catherine Allday Davis, Lewinsky's best friend, to surrender the laptop computer from which she had sent e-mail to Lewinsky. Remember that Harvard University forced its Divinity School dean to step down in 1998 for having downloaded hundreds of pornographic images onto his computer's hard drive.

It would seem that self-restraint is in order in cyberspace, given how vulnerable we are at present to surveillance (software programs that scramble what we write may well proliferate in the coming years and lessen the importance of hiding our tracks). The *Washington Post* described the peculiarly modern plight of one James Rutt, a man who scrambled to prevent us from access to his Internet past. "Rutt had spent a decade unburdening himself in an Internet chat group, and although he was happy to speak candidly in the sympathetic confines of a space that he considered a virtual corner bar, he feared that his musings about sex, politics, and his own weight problem would be used against him in his new position as the chief executive of an Internet company."[8]

Though it may prevent us from pleasurable experiences, self-control is rarely regretted. After revealing ourselves in the heat of passion, we may feel something like self-betrayal the morning after. Champions of virtue will excel at continence; consequently they will rarely, if ever, have to worry about the morning after.

Self-mastery: Overcoming the Self

How can we induce control? How can we transform a teeming mass of desires into a pillar of strength? Controlling the aggressive behavior of children, who are inclined to throw food from the high chair, to grab other kids' toys, or to scratch and bite the other toddlers, strikes most parents as an urgent necessity. Indeed, controlling the instinctual urges has struck many moralists as the foundation of character.

Aristotle speaks of bad habits in terms of addictions. Virtually anyone can be cured of his bad habits if he manages to break what may seem to be an imprisoning cycle of habit. We can overcome ourselves, he believes, if we refuse to give into temptation. Worst of all in Aristotle's eyes is the vice of self-indulgence, which he views as a result of deliberate choice:

> The man who pursues the excesses of things pleasant, or pursues to excess necessary objects, and does so by choice, for their own sake and not at all for the sake of any result distinct from them, is self indulgent; for such a man is of necessity unlikely to repent, and therefore incurable, since a man who cannot repent cannot be cured. (*Nichomachean Ethics* 1150a, 18–23)

Here, Aristotle humanely nods to the possibility that some people cannot overcome themselves, even as he stresses the immorality of self-indulgence. This is the first type of bad character; the second is slightly better. The incontinent person can resist temptation but crumbles beneath the challenge. He is

> carried away as a result of passion and contrary to the right rule—a man whom passion masters so that he does not act according to the right rule, but does not master to the extent of making him ready to believe that he ought to pursue such pleasures without reserve; this is the incontinent man, who is better than the self-indulgent man, and not bad without qualification; for the best thing in him, the first principle, is preserved. (1151a, 20–26)

The incontinent man may lose control, but not completely. He still understands the moral thing to do. He gets swept away. Raving, we'll see in chapter eight, is nothing if not self-indulgence.

Kant urges us to practice subduing stray urges *with our mental powers*: You find yourself craving chocolate cake, but you force yourself to ponder the beauty of Big Sur. What we supposedly want more than giving in to any temptation is to see ourselves standing tall. Kant's vision of human potential approaches erotic heights:

> Consider bold, overhanging and, as it were, threatening rocks, thunderclouds piling up in the sky and moving about accompanied by lightning and thunderclaps, volcanoes with all their destructive power, hurricanes with all the devastation they leave behind, the boundless ocean heaved up, the high waterfall of a mighty river, and so on. Compared to any of these, our ability to resist becomes an insignificant trifle. Yet the sight of them becomes all the more attractive the more fearful it is, provided we are in a safe place. And we like to call these objects sublime because they raise the soul's fortitude above its usual middle range and allow us to discover in ourselves an ability to resist which

is of a quite different kind, and which gives us the courage [to believe] that we could be a match for nature's seeming omnipotence.

The ability to detect what is bad for us and steer clear of its allure lifts man up above the animal kingdom and nearly makes mortals a match for God himself.[9]

This is a mental exercise, but there are physical ones as well. Consider here this passage from Laclos's *Les Liaisons Dangereuses* (1782) in which a plainly wicked woman attributes her worldly success to prowess at self-control:

> Entering the world while I was still a girl, I was imprisoned in silence and stillness. I learned how to take advantage of my prison, by observing others and reflecting on their behavior. As long as others thought me mixed up or distracted, hardly listening to the conversations from which they wished to bar me, I took pains to learn from what I was not supposed to hear.
>
> This useful curiosity which served to instruct me also taught me how to dissimulate; often forced to hide the objects of my attention from the eyes of those around me, I tried to work things to my liking; I learned from then on to assume at will that distracted look that you have so often seen on me. Encouraged by this early success, I tried to regulate in the same way the movements of my face. If I felt some chagrin, I set myself to adopting an air of serenity, even of joy; I brought the same zeal even so far as causing myself bodily pain at will while I was putting on a smiling face of pleasure. I worked with the same care but with more difficulty to hold back evidence of unexpected joy. That's how I knew how to assume this control over my body, this strength with which I have sometimes so surprised you.
>
> I was still quite young, and almost completely uninteresting: but I only had my own thoughts, and I grew furious at the thought that one could disturb me or surprise me against my will. Armed with these first weapons, I learned how to use them:

it was not enough to seal myself up, I amused myself by becoming different people; sure of my gestures, I watched my words; I regulated both, according to the circumstances, or sometimes just according to my fantasies; from that moment on, my manner of thinking was distinctively my own, and I no longer revealed any sign of what I was thinking unless it was useful to me. [Letter 81][10]

The Marquise de Merteuil teaches us something about the genesis of evil here, as well as the will to power, as she discloses in a letter the way she learned the worth (and social use) of self-control. Teachers looking for a novel through which to teach self-control could hardly do better than *Dangerous Liaisons*, in which wicked people respond to exhortations to shape up with the simple explanation, "It's beyond my control." (More on this in chapter seven.)

Concrete advice on how to strengthen our resolve, such as we find in the fictitious account above, can be extremely useful. Other examples of practicing self-control stand out for their creativity, and rising above physical limitations has produced interesting accounts of what we value. Aly Khan, the handsome son of a fabulously wealthy patriarch, spent six weeks in private training with an Egyptian physician, all in the quest of delaying and controlling ejaculation. He boasted that "he never shot until he saw the whites of their eyes" and could maintain an erection for hours, according to one of his former lovers.[11] Hollywood sex symbol Rita Hayworth became one of his wives. Mahatma Gandhi overcame his wandering eye by routinely inviting to his bed beautiful young women with whom he would then sleep naked. In the morning, he reassured his wife (and himself) that his self-control was still strong, for he had withstood the temptation to make love. He must have had a patient wife indeed.

It is not surprising that self-help books often make the best-seller lists. Far from confining themselves to high theory, philosophers will occasionally join the game and serve up recommendations such as the following—Bertrand Russell's recipe for subduing any religious impulses that may pop up in your mind:

> It is quite possible to overcome infantile suggestions of the unconscious, and even to change the contents of the unconscious, by employing the right kind of technique. Whenever you begin to feel remorse for an act which your reason tells you is not wicked, examine the causes of your feeling of remorse, and convince yourself in detail of their absurdity. Let your conscious beliefs be so vivid and emphatic that they make an impression upon your unconscious strong enough to cope with the impressions made by your nurse or your mother when you were an infant. Do not be content with an alternation between moments of rationality and moments of irrationality. Look into the irrationality closely with a determination not to respect it, and not to let it dominate you. Whenever it thrusts foolish thoughts or feelings into your consciousness, pull them up by the roots, examine them, and reject them. Do not allow yourself to remain a vacillating creature, swayed half by reason and half by infantile folly. Do not be afraid of irreverence towards the memory of those who controlled your childhood. They seemed to you then strong and wise because you were weak and foolish; now that you are neither, it is your business to examine their apparent strength and wisdom, to consider whether they deserve that reverence that from force of habit you still bestow upon them.[12]

Here again, we are urged to use reason to drive out foolishness. We must sharpen our minds so that they can grasp onto reason and stay there, despite fear. In reading Russell's words for the first time, I realized I had found justification for the fear of my devoutly Catholic parents as they sent me off to Yale as a teenager. There really was a threat to the faith, and this was it.

Earning Congratulations

How can we tell if we are succeeding in this battle against our-selves? According to Kant, observing actions is the key:

> The supreme rule is this: Give good, practical proof of yourselves in your lives by your actions; not by set prayers, but by doing good acts, by work and steadiness, and in particular by right-eousness and active benevolence towards your neighbour; then you can see whether you are good.

To defer coming to a decision, for example, shows great strength of mind, whatever that decision. It is a strong mind which can delay coming to a decision in a matter of choice until fully convinced. If I receive a letter which angers me greatly and I answer it on the spot, my answer will show much evidence of my anger, but if I can defer my reply to the follow-ing day, I will possibly approach it from a different point of view. To submit to accidents and random circumstances, Kant tells us, undermines our dignity. On the other hand, of course, if we are by personality indecisive, then we show strength when we answer such a letter with a clearly reasoned, firm reply.

Our culture reveres self-control. Since the virtue may op-erate invisibly, we may sometimes feel compelled to point out to others that we employ it. When we succeed in controlling ourselves, we may expect congratulation. In *Brideshead Revis-ited*, Waugh's 1945 novel, a neglected wife points out her long-suffering patience to her unfaithful husband:

> She talked in this way while she undressed, with an effort to ap-pear at ease; then she sat at the dressing table, ran a comb though her hair, and with her bare back towards me, looking at herself in the glass, said, "I hope you admire my self-restraint."
> "Restraint?"

"I'm not asking awkward questions. I may say I've been tormented with visions of voluptuous half-castes ever since you went away. But I determined not to ask and I haven't."[13]

One of the problems with success at self-control is the lack of visible evidence of our triumph. Others may think the reason we haven't gossiped about our colleagues for an entire week is that we've simply lost interest in office gossip.

We also understand that we have failed in some way when we override the challenge of self-control. Perhaps the only historian of the vibrator, Rachel Maines explains in the preface to her book *The Technology of Orgasm* how difficult she found concentrating on textile research whenever she would encounter advertisements for erotic devices in old newspapers and merchandise catalogs:

> As I doggedly turned the pages of *Modern Priscilla* and *Woman's Home Companion* in search of trends among the needlework patterns, my attention frequently strayed to the advertisements along the sides of the pages. It is a strong-minded historian indeed who can resist the lure of advertisements in historical periodicals; I am incapable of such iron self-discipline.[14]

Who could blame her?

In order to control our urges, we seek a critical position outside ourselves. We formulate a strategy by which to change what we dislike about ourselves, and then implement that strategy. This is the idea behind the Roman Catholic sacrament of confession. Not surprisingly, police officers have taken to inducing suspected criminals to view what happens in the examining room as a kind of cathartic release, much as Catholics do. Sharing details of your misdeed helps you evaluate it. The medieval penitentials—handbooks to which priests resorted in order to match systematically and fairly penances to sins confessed—indicate how our forebears weighed and ranked specific transgressions. Each transgression had to be overcome, and the penance in question (which was sometimes quite severe, such as hair shirts and self-flagellation) was designed to help sinners regain self-control.

There are modern examples, too, of the ways in which others expect us to overcome ourselves. Since the advent of Crest toothpaste and braces, Americans have been encouraged to smile widely and with pride. Recently, new advances in teeth whitening have reinforced this mass-cultural swell. But Victorians in England, curiously enough, considered smiling and laughing failures of self-control; in high society, sobriety was in every instance counseled. This helps to explain why we never see teeth in Victorian art.[15] Until recently in the United States, men were not supposed to cry (talk show host Phil Donahue may be credited with helping to weaken this taboo). This is not to say that men never felt the urge to cry, but that there would have been no social disapproval of crying if it had not been taken as something to be resisted, a sign of weakness, girlishness, or enfeeblement.

Women, by the same token, have been taught to control their appetites. In the 1990s, books written by women suffering from eating disorders asserted that some girls believe that they are not to eat much more than is necessary to stay alive. Lori Gottlieb offers an autobiographical account of anorexia in *Stick Figure.* Feeling as though she has lost control over her rapidly changing world, Lori focuses all her concentration on one subject: dieting. Her life narrows to a single goal—to be "the thinnest eleven-year-old on the entire planet." But once she achieves her "stick figure," Lori really sees herself for the first time in a restaurant's bathroom mirror and decides then and there to bring herself back from the brink of starvation.[16] For this young girl, overcoming herself amounted to overcoming the expectations of others.

We Are What We Do

Cutting, burning, starving, or icing one's body may appeal to some as a way of overcoming or escaping the self. Religious zealots of various stripes have relied on sensations of pain to bring them closer to God's love and forgiveness. And think of high-stress jobs and the people they attract: Air traffic controllers, brain surgeons, and international spies require a supreme ability to focus on the task at hand. Those who succeed at superhuman efforts likely derive quite a buzz. We can make a game, even a contest, out of overcoming the self. Roman Catholic nuns and priests, especially in the more ascetic orders, learn that they are not to take pride in their supreme powers of self-denial. Nonetheless, the urge to compare ourselves with others is only human, and self-abnegation contests no doubt spring up.

Another example, this one taken from *The Edge of the Bed: How Dirty Pictures Changed My Life*, centers on overcoming sexual hang-ups.[17] With honesty and humor, former Catholic schoolgirl Lisa Palac explains how she seized control of her sexuality. When she found a boyfriend's stash of pornography, her knee-jerk reaction was to tell him that if it didn't go, she would. He managed to convince her to watch a video with him; that led to another, and another. Soon she began renting her own tapes and started writing her own erotic stories. She happily abandoned some, but not all, modesty. Self-control prevented a slide down the "slippery slope."

Overcoming ourselves requires the ability to modulate what we demand or expect from the world. You must be ready to convert yourself and your whole way of seeing the world in order to pave the way for a rupture with your past. While you're at it, you might examine and evaluate every facet of who you take yourself to be, with an eye to sanding down rough or embarrassing spots.

What is the goal of self-overcoming? Self-actualization. We become ourselves by stepping over base urges. We find ourselves in making our behavior correspond to the ideal we have set for ourselves. When my experience of myself matches up with my ideal of myself, then I am truly, sincerely, finally, authentically *me*.

However, authenticity has baffled and bewitched philosophers for millennia. Everyone seems to agree that it is a good idea, although there is confusion about the desired state. When are we most genuinely ourselves? in moments when we deny ourselves? in the confessional, when we bear down on our shortcomings and misdeeds? in psychoanalysis, when we strive to expose our deepest corners and hiding spaces? Is it true that self-deception impedes our efforts to become genuinely ourselves; does self-esteem facilitate the trek? The questions remain perplexing, for only we can know whether or not we have become genuinely ourselves.

If it's true that we are what we eat, then it might also be said that we are what we want. But this analogy is not perfect, for there are plenty of foods we might want to eat but purposely don't (those high in fat or sodium, namely). And so, even though certain temptations may call out to us, it would be misleading to link our identities to those sworn-off temptations. It would be more accurate to say that we are what we do and, as well, the strength we summon in the face of what's bad for us.

We can strengthen our self-control through a peculiar variety of exercises. We know how high the moral stakes can sometimes loom, and so we flirt with boundaries. Just as we avoid premature satiation while eating, pacing our intake of food we enjoy, so as to prolong the pleasure, so do we keep one eye on the point of no return while we push the envelope. One false move, and we could lose a job or a spouse. And yet we may feel entitled, even compelled, to explore the tipping point. We know that taking a single, curious step toward the forbidden does not mean that we will automatically slide into the verboten. And so fear of the tipping point itself can drive us to examine precisely how far we can go before falling off the cliff.

chapter six

The Men of UVa

"*A man who is ashamed to show or name the penis is wrong. [Instead] of being anxious to hide it, man ought to display it, with honor.*" —LEONARDO DA VINCI

SO FAR I HAVE CONSIDERED MORE OR LESS OBVIOUS IN-stances of losing self-control, or examples of how others worry that we are harming ourselves. Here I will turn to a much sub-tler illustration of how we may think we harm ourselves while others disagree. As before, shifting cultural ideas of what is bad for us serves as the backdrop for my central point: That tire-some self-control fanatic, the prude, is back, just when you'd least expect him.

American teenagers and college students find themselves routinely accused of lacking self-discipline: they spend an ap-palling amount of time watching television, they are over-weight to a startling degree, they become sexually active much too young, and they resist homework. One thing college stu-dents would appear to excel at is maintaining their privacy. Not just in their bedrooms at home or their dormitories at school—twenty-somethings remain permanently alert to the possibility that others might see them naked. Even their own peers, of the same sex. In this chapter I explore the curious phenomenon of unnecessary self-control.

The men of the University of Virginia, or UVa, as it's called, will show us what they believe is bad for them. And a partic-ular man from UVa will illustrate the oddity of self-control, namely why and when we say no to ourselves. This man, B., shielded himself from view in the locker room during the week but grabbed the spotlight in a strip club on the weekend.

Few young men contemplating their first full-time job consider professional stripping. Taking it all off, either on the big stage or in the men's locker room, can signal high risk to one's self-regard: how does one's body look to others? is it adequate? attractive? not so good? does it matter? who is even looking? It's not so hard to understand someone shying away from public undressing, but hiding in the locker room? How can something so apparently trifling seem so tremendous? What is the point of self-control in the locker room, or anywhere for that matter? Self-control masks fear, and fear can take the most surprising twists and turns.

Locker-Room Culture

The only stripper I have known stopped changing in the locker room just as he was planning to begin his job. B. graduated from the University of Virginia and moved to an American city, where he now dances on a bar several nights a week. A friend of mine, having heard a report of B.'s employment, went to the bar and, sure enough, spied B.'s act. The Web site for the bar features flattering pictures of B., wearing only a smile.[1]

The first time B. spoke to me, I was taken aback by his size. We stood in the showers, a mere twelve feet from the pool in which I had just been swimming. Cautiously, he befriended me, a stranger. Months later, he began seeking me out regularly to discuss frustration with his secret boyfriend, a law student who swam with me a few times a week. L., the boyfriend, had been a superb swimmer in college, qualifying for the Olympic Trials.

Swimmers tend to frequent the Aquatics and Fitness Center, the newest of UVa's four gyms. With a beautiful fifty-meter pool and an expansive weight room built in the style of a Victorian train station, the AFC draws faculty and students from early in the morning until just before midnight. The busy locker room can accommodate well over two hundred patrons. You can tell who the students are: They are the ones who avoid the shower (sometimes the locker room altogether) and who hide behind towels while changing in front of their lockers. They sometimes stumble and fall while trying to squirm out of their clothes without exposing what remains hidden beneath a bathing suit or gym shorts.

What are they so afraid of? How could the passing glance of a stranger or fellow student harm them? The 1991 film *Europa, Europa* depicts a young Jewish boy in Nazi Germany who lives in terror that someone may see his circumcised penis; such exposure would identify him as a Jew, instead of the Aryan Hitler Youth he pretends to be.[2] Based on a true story, the film supplies a good answer to why a man would conceal himself in an atmosphere of rabid anti-Semitism. But twenty-first-century American undergraduates down at the gym?

Fear of being identified as a gay man may be the answer. I can't help but think of the Morehouse College incident as highly unusual, though. In 2003 a student, Aaron Price, beat another student, Gregory Love, with a baseball bat in a dormitory bathroom. Price felt outraged that Love had glanced his way in the showers. Mr. Love, who suffered a fractured skull, later explained that he had not been wearing his glasses and mistook Mr. Price for his roommate. Price was convicted of assault and battery charges and could spend forty years in prison.[3] Personally, I don't think UVa students are at risk of such barbarism.

Maybe they fear that other men will "kiss and tell"—see and then speak to mutual friends. Rumors do spread. The men of UVa may dread reports which overstate or, more likely, understate what they would prefer to shield beneath a towel. Put yourself in their place: Could you stand the idea of someone bruiting about your private measurements, much in the way the emcee for the Miss America pageant will introduce a new contestant by reciting the size of her hips and bust?

Maybe the men who hide, "hiders," fear tainting. Although the UVa hardly qualifies as a gay mecca, a few men do live openly as sexual nonconformists. A young man from the provinces, arriving at this relatively isolated university, may fear the gaze of other men who just might desire him. Being seen by unknown men might compromise you or expose you to danger. Think of Susannah and the elders, Bathsheba and David, the bathhouses of ancient Greece, or Hollywood prison movies. The scenario of a naked young person arousing the lust of a more experienced man is well known in our culture. Being ogled isn't much fun, granted, but simply ignoring an unwanted glance should steer young men back into safe waters.

Or maybe they fear being photographed unwittingly. Perhaps they have read news accounts of other college men being captured naked on film without ever suspecting the presence of a camera. In the late 1990s, the FBI investigated the appearance of a videotape of wrestlers from the University of Pennsylvania who had participated in the national championships, held at Northwestern University. The videotape enraged coaches and administrators at Penn, showing as it did Penn wrestlers undressing, showering, and unclothed in weigh-in areas. It seems that men posing as athletic trainers had concealed small video recorders in gym bags, strategically placed around the locker room. The videotapes were distributed by a Web site called Young Studs Online, which charged $7.95 a month and boasted: "We proudly feature the Internet's largest collection on the Web of hidden camera locker room photos!" Subsequent videotapes were sold on the Internet under titles such as *Straight Off the Mat* and *Voyeur Time*. The FBI eventually succeeded. In December 2002, a federal judge in Chicago ordered a group of individuals and video companies to pay more than $500 million to forty-six athletes who were filmed in college without their knowledge in dormitory showers or locker rooms.[4]

Fearing an invasion of privacy such as the Penn wrestlers suffered surely constitutes a legitimate worry. But I don't think that's what motivates the men of UVa, relatively few of whom are serious athletes. The men of UVa conform to a certain locker room culture, one they may have learned in high school. At my public high school in rural Pennsylvania, showers were obligatory after gym classes twice a week. No matter how much you disliked showering naked en masse in the 1980s, you had no choice. It may be that boys who disliked showering naked in high school gym class abandon the practice as soon as they arrive at UVa. In any event, at UVa undergraduate men enter a streaking culture that clashes with locker room prudishness.

Ask any teacher who lives on the Lawn, the historic center of UVa, and you'll hear the same complaint. Night after night, raucous groups of undergraduates cavort naked in public. True, it may be night time, but visibility remains. The flashlights and searchlights other students shine on streakers help bystanders observe the action. The student newspaper has published pictures of mobile students liberated from clothes. Try as they may, policemen have failed to squelch the tradition of running the distance of the Lawn naked at least once before graduating.

Statistically, it must be that some of the same students who laboriously hide themselves in the (male only) locker rooms expose themselves publicly at night. How can this be? What difference in risk level do students feel? What is it about a locker room that triggers a heightened sense of danger? Why does self-control ramp up locker room behavior but not public frolicking?

The men of UVa conduct themselves much as Victorian upper-class women are, at least in legend, said to have done. The gym towel of today is the equivalent of those underskirts, slips, and corsets with which Victorian ladies protected their honor. But unlike women living in nineteenth-century England, most UVa students are American-born and used to watching scantily clad people cavorting on MTV or in the movies. American adolescents today can, with minimal effort, find films and television shows featuring nearly naked people. Paradoxically, at least in the case of the UVa sports center, culture of nudity requires prudishness, or instinctive self-censorship in unnecessary circumstances. Perhaps here the media molds culture less than we expected.

Maybe men are not alone in their locker room modesty. Not long ago, a friend visited me and, over dinner back home, chuckled at the locker room antics of UVa women. My friend gave me to understand that these women take similar pains to hide themselves in the dressing room, unlike female students at Stanford, where she teaches law. And so it seems that the locker room cultures for men and women are in synch at UVa. Some of the UVa women will be or are already customers at Victoria's Secret, a popular lingerie store that reached into yesterday's pornography in order to transform today's mainstream fashion. Commercial photographers report robust business in the field of "boudoir photography": Women who work as lawyers, accountants, or corporate moguls-to-be pay hefty fees to pose before the camera in their own bedrooms, made up to look like *Playboy* centerfolds.[5] But UVa women comport themselves like nuns in the locker room.

Culture colors the need to control who sees our bodies and in what contexts. Ethnic groups may inculcate different notions of modesty in adolescents. The American fiction writer Sandra Cisneros began a meditation on her Catholic upbringing with an anecdote about locker room anxiety:

> In high school I marveled at how white women strutted around the locker room, nude as pearls, as unashamed of their brilliant bodies as the Nike of Samothrace. Maybe they were hiding terrible secrets like bulimia or anorexia, but to my naive eye then, I thought of them as women comfortable in their skin.
>
> You could always tell us Latinas. We hid when we undressed, modestly facing a wall, or, in my case, dressing in a bathroom stall.[6]

We are left to wonder if Cisneros still sees Caucasian women strutting naked around the gym locker room. Another question to tackle, one for which there is no room here, would be why American women seem to accompany one another regularly to the public restroom to gossip, to chaperone one another, and so on.[7]

In chapter three I discussed the pride Elisabeth Eaves came to feel as a stripper. Eaves compares the dressing room used by her fellow performers to a locker room:

> It wasn't like a gym locker room, either, because in those most women were furtive in their nudity, dressing and undressing with quick utilitarian movements and not a hint of pride. It was rare that I had seen a naked woman in a locker room looking casual or relaxed. Far more often I had seen women swathe themselves in towels and try to change awkwardly underneath, or simply duck into toilet stalls.[8]

The women's locker room scenes from *Carrie* (1976), *Personal Best* (1982), or *Sex and the City* (e.g., Season III, Episode 3) might be a mere projection of male fantasy, or perhaps an indication of how much locker room culture has evolved since the 1980s. American women naked together has become a historical memory, it seems, a relic of the twentieth century. Just like the men of UVa.

The New York Athletic Club

Dropping our guard has a lot to do with self-respect and how we allow others to see us. Through the Judaeo-Christian centuries, modesty has governed women with a stronger arm than men. Women have not traditionally flocked to private sports clubs as men have; opportunities for group nudity have been fewer and expectations for self-shrouding have been higher.

It is largely in the religious sphere that expectations for

male modesty have flowered, but even here, comparatively less so than for women. The book of Genesis, for example, recounts Noah's fury over having been caught unawares (Genesis 9:20–27). Drunk, Noah falls asleep, inadvertently exposes his ungirded loins, and enslaves his son Ham (and Ham's entire family) for having chanced upon the sight. Social inferiors, we learn from this story, are not allowed to see their superiors naked (think here of the dramatic scene in di Lampedusa's novel *The Leopard,* when the timid priest accidentally walks in while the virile father of the wealthy family he serves is taking a bath).

In any event, Judaism, Christianity, and Islam alike have each promulgated sexual morals the underside of which implies that physical modesty behooves women and men alike. Perhaps Catholics alone have tolerated, even encouraged, artistic depictions of nudity. Particularly in Mediterranean countries, Catholic churches feature crucifixes on which the Christ's gorgeously muscular body languishes almost completely naked. Leo Steinberg has illuminated the sexuality of Christ in Renaissance art, both the prominence given the Savior's genitals and our refusal in subsequent centuries to notice them.[9] Paintings of St. Sebastian, a popular saint shown tied to a column and pierced with arrows, similarly showcase the flesh of a marvelously virile youth. And from time to time, paintings of St. Lucy or St. Agnes will tantalize the viewer with barely covered breasts.

A Catholic myself, locker rooms have figured prominently in my life. I began swimming competitively at the age of ten. Practices several times a week and Saturday meets drew me to the local YMCA. Unlike the men of UVa, no one ever arrived at the pool wearing a bathing suit under street clothes; he would have been taunted by a sneering mob of boys. Years later, I can still recall the insults of the other little boys when, after one of my first practices, I tried to remove my suit from beneath my towel. I learned right away that this wasn't cool; only a sissy boy would hide in the locker room, and no one wanted that branding. The impulse to hide had seemed natural to me: Growing up in a house run by devout Catholic parents, there was never any nudity.

Off to college I went at age eighteen. Yale's locker room culture in the 1980s differed little from what I had grown accustomed to in rural Pennsylvania. Some of the guys kept their suits on during the team shower after twice-a-day workouts, and some did not. No one, however, hid behind a towel in our team locker room. We all knew without being told that squeamishness would evoke jeers from the rest of the team. After our late afternoon workouts, the crew team would often end up in the showers when we did. I sometimes wondered what the crew jocks, always naked, thought of those of us swimmers who kept their suits on. In any event, no one ever said anything.

After graduation I took a job at Morgan Stanley, a Wall Street investment bank. The gyms of New York City struck me as overcrowded and overpriced, and pools were hard to come by. I couldn't imagine life without swimming and reassessed my future in a city I was beginning to love. An older Yale contact then urged me to try out for the swim team at the New York Athletic Club, a men's club located on posh Central Park South. Once I made it on the NYAC swim team, I gained entrance to one of the nicest gyms in Manhattan (it was actually an enormous social club that included a spacious gym) for free.

My audition hadn't worried me much. I had agreed to meet one of the team leaders on a street corner outside the NYAC early one evening. He took me into the club, past the vigilant guards. Making small talk all the way, we ventured to the locker room, where I began unloading my bag. I placed a suit and goggles on the bench and continued chatting. He looked toward the bench and said with some surprise that I wouldn't need "that." Confused, I asked him what he meant. He clarified that I would not need a suit. I took this as a weak joke and smiled obligingly. He then told me that he meant it, that not only did I not need a suit, I would not be permitted into the pool with one.

My mind raced. I thought this was a sort of initiation prank; this, it occurred to me, must be the kind of antics played in college fraternities. It occurred to me that I might just leave the NYAC then and there, but I decided to stay. If a group of frat boys wanted to laugh at me as I walked naked to the pool, I could certainly endure their laughing. I would rise above their silliness.

Sure enough, the team leader approached the pool naked as well. I felt very strange and wondered what the breathless group of frat boys waiting for us would say. To my surprise, we entered the pool area, around which fifty or so naked businessmen walked and talked casually. Clearly, I had reached an unusual place.

After swimming a naked time trial, I was quickly invited to join the team. Then I was asked why I seemed surprised by NYAC culture: Had I never heard that nudity was enforced by the club? To the surprise of the other guys, I hadn't. The enforced nudity seemed quite odd to me, but I later learned that men of my father's generation all swam naked at YMCAs around the country. At Yale, the swim team had also trained naked, up until coeducation in 1969. I was told that I would gradually get used to pool nudity, that I would even come to enjoy it.

I did. So much so that I chuckled when, in the early 1990s, the city of New York mandated that the NYAC either admit women as members or start paying higher taxes. The NYAC hired lawyers and fought hard to maintain the old ways, which came down to obligatory nudity on the third floor. The NYAC eventually lost its legal bid, and membership plummeted. Members were apparently not interested in a club that forbade nudity.

It was at the NYAC that I lost my prudishness. I had no choice, really, and so I empathize somewhat with the men of UVa.

Jogging Shirtless

UVa hardly figures as an evangelical Christian bulwark. Male joggers pop up everywhere in warm weather; often they forego shirts. This does not strike me as so odd, a man who will jog shirtless but hide behind a towel in the locker room. For I had done roughly the same thing before the New York Athletic Club. As a competitive swimmer, I wore practically nothing to practice and meets, and yet I always felt dressed. Today it seems no one can mount a bike without first slipping into spandex; the same swimmers who do not feel comfortable wearing a Speedo racing suit to the pool (and American coaches complain about the rising number of boys who resist these suits) jump into spandex as if it were concealing sackcloth.

What if it could be proven that our grandfathers were more comfortable with male nudity than we ourselves are today? What would that tell us? Just as public morals relax, private ones contract.

Time spent in the locker room now seems a necessary evil to many sweaty undergraduates at UVa, an unpleasant step before and after exercise. Self-regulation asserts its urgency in a most unlikely place.

For centuries, men and women throughout Europe and England undressed together at the public baths. Same-sex nudity in the name of cleanliness does not seem to have bothered anyone. According to Tacitus, it was excessive bathing that brought down the Roman Empire. He protested that at midday, all officers of a particular unit in Gaul were at the baths. Even today, Americans come home from European vacations giddy with tales of beaches on which most women lie topless.

Getting naked with other people signifies intimacy to many of us. How do we feel about passing on the street strangers who have seen us naked? For many, this is a matter of no importance. But for plenty of others, it is. The American public is barred from access to the notorious "physique photographs" of some of our better known countrymen. Throughout the 1950s and 1960s, undergraduates at Yale, Harvard, Princeton, Smith, Wellesley, and a few other schools had to pose naked, for a photographer who would scan subsequent pictures for clues about health and intelligence. Who knows, maybe when we reach our sixties we'll regret never having posed naked while young. For now, we chuckle at the insistence of Diane Sawyer, George W. Bush, and Hillary Clinton and others that no one ever be allowed access to this curious collection.

A more interesting question might be, How do we feel about passing in the hallway colleagues who have seen pictures of us naked? In chapter three I discussed the professional dilemma of Christian Curry. In 1998 New York City newspapers gleefully bandied about a story of a twenty-four-year-old analyst at the patrician Wall Street firm of Morgan Stanley Dean Witter. Christian Curry had posed for the gay men's magazine *Playguy* while fully erect. Several days after word spread through the office, the firm let go the analyst, accusing him of extensive expense-account fraud. Curry in turn filed a billion-dollar lawsuit against the firm, protesting its racial discrimination (he is African-American) and homophobia (even though he insists he is heterosexual). The firm's top lawyer resigned over fallout from the controversy. Under pressure, another senior lawyer quit as well.

Christian Curry had posed for the pictures three years earlier, while an undergraduate at Columbia. Then an aspiring model, he admitted he had posed partly out of vanity. No doubt he had understood at a young age the force of the photoerotic, and serving as the stimulus for the fantasies of others appealed to him.

Just as Catholics for centuries feared looking on artistic representations of Christ's sexuality, so do many UVa students now fear looking upon the manhood of their classmates. Why? Perhaps they fear they will enjoy the vision. Writing in *Civilization and Its Discontents,* Freud asserted that the sight of genitals is "always exciting," even though they are "hardly ever judged to be beautiful."[10] It is one thing to expose one's chest and abs for public view; it is quite another to unveil the full monty.

A Man's Body

Penis jokes pop up everywhere, it seems. On the playground, in the movies, across popular magazines, we find snickering over the small and reverence for the large. In *The Godfather* (1972), an ode to old-time masculinity, women gather around a wedding table to trade secrets about what they discovered on their wedding nights. In *The Godfather, Part II* (1974), the references are more graphic, and the New York gang attends an underworld exhibition of a naked man whose endowment draws gasps from those present. The American public heard a good deal about a porn movie character named "Long Dong Silver" during the painful Senate hearings before which Clarence Thomas ascended to the Supreme Court in 1991. The Austin Powers spy spoof movies (beginning in 1997) include a number of stupidly funny scenes concerning the evolving size of Austin's penis. Mel Brooks gloriously joked about the Monster's endowment in *Young Frankenstein* (1974). And then there was Mark Wahlberg's character's bittersweet triumph at the end of *Boogie Nights* (1997): a frontal view of his huge penis.

Truman Capote once dismissed America's most famous family as overrated. "What I don't understand is why everybody said the Kennedys were so sexy," he groused. Letting the cat out of the bag, he revealed:

> I know a lot about cocks—I've seen an awful lot of them—and if you put all the Kennedys together, you wouldn't have a good one. I used to see Jack in Palm Beach. I had a little guest cottage with its own private beach, and he would come down so he could

swim in the nude. He had absolutely nothin'! Bobby was the same way—I don't know how he had all those children. As for Teddy—forget it.[11]

In this age of idolizing celebrities, no famous man is safe from speculation. And in the futurist age of designer babies, hopeful parents may one day be able to specify more than blond hair and blue eyes when ordering a son.

The legendary playboy Porfirio Rubirosa (1909–65) rose from rags to riches in the 1930s, leaving the Dominican Republic for the United States to marry Doris Duke, the daughter of the richest man in the world. Duke's biographer details one corner of Rubirosa's extraordinary charm:

> His sexual technique was widely discussed and his penis was allegedly neither hard nor soft, but suspended in a state of retarded ejaculation. "Toujours prêt," as the French say. The technical word is "priapic." Doris later used another description. "It was always numb," she confided to a friend. His penis was also of such proportion that waiters in Parisian restaurants began referring to the giant peppermills as "Rubirosas." Jimmy Cromwell had another name for him: "Rubber Hosa."[12]

What man would appreciate being teased or ridiculed in this way? More than you might think.

Penis references can still shock and offend others. The reviewer for the *New York Times Book Review* objected to the very mention of Rubirosa's measurement in the Doris Duke biography. And an American philosophy professor confessed her astonishment at the link between penis humor and racism on her highly selective New England campus. Asian males there reported the disparaging references made by fellow students about the allegedly modest endowments of Asian men (these comments circulated among the wrestling team one afternoon in the showers after a college match). The Wesleyan professor objected strenuously to something she insisted should not be dismissed as mere teasing.[13]

Any male undergraduate in America will know something about this teasing. Jokes of this sort spring from male-only environments; although such jokes have nothing to do with male-directed sexual desire, gay gatherings will highlight the issue. And so we might look to the gay world for an increase in the frequency of this concern about size. In detailing the burgeoning popularity of bath houses for gay men in the early 1970s, Douglas Sadownick points out limits to the euphoria inside New York and California establishments:

> Some gay men behaved in brutally rude ways to each other. Men deemed too fat or too old were treated as pariahs; they in turn could be seen to paw younger men without permission. Those whose dicks did not measure up perhaps suffered worst of all.[14]

The men of UVa, living pretty far from a gay subculture, probably know little if anything of bath house customs. Yet undergraduates do understand the premium placed on size. John Munder Ross, recalling his adolescent days, has written in *The Sadomasochism of Everyday Life*, "I shudder to think about the damage that my cronies and I inflicted on those schoolmates less fortunate in their endowment than ourselves."[15] Being made fun of is rarely fun. In any arena, the stinging realization that one simply cannot compete will require management (through telling oneself one simply does not care to compete, or through trivializing the competition, for example). To compensate for feelings of inferiority, young men may plunge themselves into tests of power in the classroom, on the playing field, or in driving fast cars.

A man's body changes during puberty no less than it alters the world around him. Writing in Book II of the *Confessions*, Augustine remarks on the joy his father felt one day at the baths; the father crowed that his son was "growing toward manhood and showing the signs of burgeoning youth." Augustine understood he had achieved something important. Competitive types find new venues in which to show up each other. Many adolescent boys eventually take to weight lifting; a barrage of cultural cues stirs their vanity and forms their sense of masculinity. In most gyms, whether private or university ones, you can spot men showing off muscles upstairs on the gym floor. UVa is no exception here. Body pressure may unite men to their beleaguered sisters, who no doubt face even more of it. A woman's body is on display almost everywhere; indeed, young women will report being mocked by other young women if they don't dress stylishly, that is to say, wear tight-fitting clothing. The size of a clothed woman's bust is rarely a mystery, whereas the size of a clothed man's privates almost always is.

The path-breaking art historian Johann Joachim Winckelmann (1717–68) celebrated the naked male body. Winckelmann's *History of Ancient Art* deified the statues of naked Greek teenagers, most of them athletes. Perhaps under the spell of Winckelmann, Goethe claimed that male beauty exceeded female beauty. "In his essays on Wincklemann (1805), Goethe wrote that nature had provided him with everything that makes and graces a man."[16] Apparently Goethe bragged justifiably; in his dazzling history of swimming, *Haunts of the Black Masseur,* Charles Strawson relays the news that Goethe was "physically as well endowed as he was mentally."[17] It is, after all, important to give credit where credit is due.

Speculating on how men think is hard, and it is hard to imagine how hiding undergraduates would react to an art class in which they were instructed to draw the nude body of a model in their midst, much less how they would respond to the countless examples of nudes culled from the history of painting and sculpture. And yet it seems reasonable to maintain that the men of UVa would go on hiding.

The gay liberation movement has triggered certain cultural shifts, and Americans are still coming to grips with the idea of gays serving in the military or taking part in the Boy Scouts.[18] Soldiers interviewed on national news programs have openly worried that gay men may watch them change clothes, silently grabbing masturbation fodder, images to hold on to mentally and then savor privately. A man's body is off limits today.

Locker-Room Intimacy

The pageantry of American masculinity today must include clothes. Not long ago, men used to exercise together naked, shower together naked, and stroll around the locker room naked, oblivious to or in denial of the erotic potential of such camaraderie. Then, everyone was heterosexual.

The *New York Times* reported a curious cultural shift in 1996: American high school students had stopped taking showers after gym class.[19] No union banded together to organize the movement, no charismatic leader arose to lead the charge against the establishment. Boys and girls decided on their own that public nakedness was not kosher. The American Civil Liberties Union (ACLU) leapt to their aid and argued for the protection of civil rights of teenagers, targeting a Pennsylvania school district that enforced a mandatory shower policy. Responding to a reporter's questions, one incredulous student asked, "Standing around together naked? Oh no, man—people would feel really uncomfortable about that."

Exhibitionism stands as roughly the opposite of what motivates hiders, who fear fatal contamination in the locker room. For hiders, the gaze of others amounts to a sexual crime, a violation of privacy, even of security. It is almost as if other men can secrete a poison—AIDS? bisexuality?—through the eyes. Ocular stakes can run high, for we invest the act of seeing with great significance. The legendary art critic Ruskin once said, "The greatest thing a human soul ever does in this world is to see something, and tell what it saw in a plain way.... To see clearly is poetry, prophecy, and religion—all in one."[20]

Privacy concerns all of us, and democracies work to guarantee that citizens will enjoy it. The modern media has given us unprecedented access into the private lives of others, particularly celebrities. Michael Jackson and Bill Clinton, both accused of sexual misconduct in differing circumstances in the 1990s, had to endure the media trumpeting accounts of the size, shape, and coloration of their members. Nowadays, the world is a locker room.

The psychiatrist Willard Gaylin observed in 1992, "When I first started practicing in New York, I became aware that the vast majority of my male patients assumed they had a penis smaller than average." And so the modern world only becomes more competitive. Later on the same page, Gaylin captures the anxiety of locker room curiosity, "When he observes the penis of another, it is with a surreptitious glance that must be fleeting and quick, lest the observation be seen as either an invitation, or worse, an assault."[21] Lingering in the locker room may raise suspicions, even though the voyeuristic TV cameras which roam through locker rooms after football games picture apparently naked men basking in each other's company.

The idea that we can assault others with our eyes, as opposed to merely offend them, fascinates me. Just as prurience degrades sex to mere sensual gratification, so does prudery relegate the male body to the gutter. We can question whether the naked body, male or female, is ever emptied of its erotic content (in a doctor's office, on a public beach, or in a locker room). In my unscientific, unobtrusive observations, I detect a resurgence of Victorian attitudes that the body is something shameful or sinful. I wonder about the coping processes of hiders, their successful social adaptation, and positive self-attributions.

Hiders prevail in the locker room. Unlike run-of-the-mill non-hiders, hiders and exhibitionists share a preoccupation with seeing and being seen that can make changing clothes feel like losing control of oneself.

Self-control without Cause

We succeed at self-control in direct proportion to risk. The more we risk losing in the face of a threat, the more likely we will manage to control ourselves. There is something odd about people who exercise self-control when there is no need to. Guarding the self from others, while not exactly self-control, points up an intriguing manifestation of caring for the self.

Today, nudity seems to diminish *bonhommie* in the UVa locker room. What an odd place for old-fashioned modesty to blossom, the men's locker room! At a time when Americans lament the nudity and violence that saturate commercial advertisements and the media generally, young men become shrinking violets. Body modesty is one arena in which male undergraduates do not fail at self-control; it seems safe to conclude they sense serious risk in the locker room.

A man cannot control the size of all parts of his body. True, penile enlargement surgery has risen dramatically in frequency, but for most men, what they have will remain all they have. A man can, however, control the exposure of his body. Why he should choose to regulate this exposure among other men raises questions about personal identity and the importance of what we care about.

Fear may motivate hiders, or is it modesty or possibly shame? I have never dared to ask one of the hiding men in the locker room why they do it; such a question, coming from a teacher, would verge on sexual harassment. Not that I think I would get an answer anyway—a prude would shy away. What is interesting is that so many undergraduate men police themselves in this arena; they mail fail at self-control when it comes to drinking, drugs, completing requirements for courses, and safe sex, but they succeed at hiding themselves. Hiding really matters to them.

Shrouding oneself from the gaze of other men seems oddly out of place in the twenty-first century. Exposing your naked body to your peers in a locker room is a little thing of no importance, we might think, and yet it represents a defeat, a moment invested with dread. For one reason or another, little things mean a lot.

Self-Harm in the Locker Room

Tainting inspires fear. Think of classes or castes: In the age of Empire and, in fact, long afterwards, many Brits didn't want to mix with their colonial (and postcolonial) "subjects." For centuries, the aristocracy worried that just being seen with lower classes would dirty them. Religious people didn't want to see pornographic images—ever—because they worried that just a glimpse could taint them. Well into the twentieth century, Roman Catholics believed that it was a sin even to enter a mosque or a synagogue; just being in such a space would harm or taint them.

Instead of working among the poor or the sick (think of Mother Teresa or AIDS patients), many well-meaning souls prefer just to send cash donations. The fear of contagion, in addition to busy schedules, leads people to keep their distance.

In a short story entitled "The Term Paper Artist," David Leavitt describes the interaction between a pious Mormon undergraduate from UCLA who has turned to an openly gay man for help on a writing project. Nervous over the interaction, the student reaches for his wallet and, opening it, brandishes a photograph of the woman he intends to marry. The gay man understands the threat of contamination he poses to the undergraduate: "Then he put the picture away, as if continued exposure to my gaze might blight it."[22] So do undergraduates at

UVa fear that the gaze of other men might pollute them. One doesn't want to be the sort of guy who runs naked through other people's yards, and one doesn't want to be known as the sort of guy who gets naked in the locker room.

Many guys worry that, by undressing in the locker room, they will send a covert message that they are gay. These guys understand on some level that they would be harming themselves by allowing us to assume homosexuality.

Homophobia has become more covert, more insidious. Lots of guys now say that it is fine to be gay, but inside they fear gay guys. And so the rubber hits the road in the locker room— straight guys hide from the gaze of strangers, who might just be gay. Straight guys fear that the stray look of a gay guy will stain and leave an awful trace. It's a visceral reaction, one that speaks volumes to homophobia and the idea of protecting the self from potential harm.

Another possibility presents itself in "hiders," or men who avoid the UVa locker room altogether: they may disappoint the possibly gay men walking around the male venue. It's not so much that you may fail to measure up genitally as that you may fail to arouse much interest at all generally. The possibly gay men in the locker room may pass you over, just as they do women. This kind of failure may pack more of a punch than the other, namely dropping your guard momentarily and ending up tainted by the glance of a man who privately covets you.

LOCKER ROOM CULTURE INTRODUCES A MUCH MORE SUBtle form of self-harm than cutting or masturbation or crash diets or smoking. Superstition and anxiety can certainly be bad for us as well, and this meditation on a moment of the day (that is, shower time at the gym) suggests that what really needs managing these days is not our diet or pastimes but rather our sexual reputation. What's bad for us is the circulating report that we allow those of our sex to see us naked. Self-control can show up in the most unexpected venues.

UVa, a school cramped for space, might do well to consider doing away with the men's locker room. It is no longer needed by many. Male patrons could simply change clothes in a small bathroom, then leave their things in hallway lockers. A few showers on the deck of the pool could accommodate both men and women, all of whom would wash up in bathing suits. The space now used for the men's locker room could be converted into a classroom. Not so far in the future, students may question their teachers in the converted space, "Is it really true that men used to get naked here, together?" Teachers who can remember will respond in the affirmative. "How weird!" students will marvel. "What were they thinking?"

chapter seven

Beyond Our Control

CHILDREN AND ADOLESCENTS START AN ESTIMATED 70,000 fires each year in the United States, causing at least 300 deaths, 2,000 injuries, and more than $300 million in damage. Professionals who staff the 150 fire-setter-treatment centers nationwide report that many children explain that their fire-setting urges are simply overwhelming. Compounding the threat to public safety are parents who will do anything to cover up for their dangerous children.[1]

Certain feats would seem to lie beyond our control, despite herculean efforts to chart our own course. This insight supplies us all with a ready excuse. Like the characters in *Dangerous Liaisons,* we can simply respond to those who scold us, "Sorry, it's beyond my control." We can't blame anyone for failing to grab something beyond his or her reach, and we can never know for sure whether our expectations of others are appropriate. The limits of our personal power color and shape our notion of what it is to be human.

Even as it labors to provide tools to predict the unpredictable and to control the uncontrollable, modern science has confirmed the limits of our control. Here I look briefly at violent behavior and clinical depression.

Crime and Self-control

Whether we have a real self and what it looks like (fragmented or unified?) has long bothered philosophers and psychologists. If a criminal's real self is rotten, there is not much point in urging him to find himself or working to rehabilitate him in prison. He needs a trip to reeducation camp, a personality makeover. Plato believed that to know the good is to do the good, which is to say that we don't commit crimes and misdemeanors because we are bad people, but because we haven't been taught yet how to behave (what to strive for, etc.). Quite the optimist, Plato would disagree with psychoanalysts and novelists who argue that some people just don't work hard enough to do the right thing.

Why wouldn't you work hard enough to do the right thing? Theories of crime point out how seductive it can be to step out of line, to try to get something for nothing. According to Michael Gottfredson and Travis Hirschi, criminals don't necessarily lack self-control; often criminal acts are committed during low water marks of self-control. Gottfredson and Hirschi describe criminal acts as providing:

· immediate gratification of desires
· easy or simple gratification of desires
· exciting, risky, or thrilling sensations
· quick rewards from minimal skill or planning
· genuine satisfaction at contemplating the pain or discomfort of the victim.[2]

They also point out, curiously, that "people lacking self-control will also tend to pursue immediate pleasures that are not criminal: They will tend to smoke, drink, use drugs, gamble, have children out of wedlock, and engage in illicit sex." This is curious because, morally speaking, some of these habits do qualify as "criminal."

One very practical benefit of insisting that everyone develop his self-control is the likely reduction of crime in a society. One disadvantage must be that we begin to expect the worst of smokers, drinkers, and the like. For Gottfredson and Hirschi come close to describing "impulsive, insensitive, physical (as opposed to mental), risk-taking, short-sighted, and nonverbal" people as criminals in the making. They also express less optimism about the potential for rehabilitation than does Plato, whose *Republic* is, at base, a picture of supremely self-controlled souls living in harmony.

One great weakness of Plato's position is the increasingly compelling case that some people really can't help themselves. Clinical depression is not a crime, nor is alcoholism. And yet we thought well into the 1960s that individuals could be blamed for both. What does the culture shift in these areas say about our attitude toward self-control? Although Westerners still tend to believe that self-control can stop crime, medical advances undermine that confidence.

Biological Revolution

The control paradigm is being supplanted. Much of the ancient world thought of passions (for example, love and anger) as forces over which we have little power. Many centuries later, John Locke strengthened this paradigm. In his *Essay Concerning Human Understanding* (II.xxi.4) he reasoned: "For when the ball obeys the motion of a billiard stick, it is not any action of the ball, but bare passion." For many years we similarly thought of emotions much as we do religious callings, as undertaken without choice. Sex writer Lisa Palac reveals how, as a Catholic schoolgirl, she internalized her religious culture:

> Because of my profane thoughts, I feared that I'd become a nun, as a punishment. That would straighten me out good. On Career Day at school, joining the convent was always presented as a fine choice. "But not everyone is chosen to do the Lord's work," the

sisters would say, and go on to tell us how one day they just "got the calling" and that was that. "God, please don't pick me," I'd whisper over and over, bowing my head.[3]

This view makes some sense, as it helps us understand why some people get angry more frequently than do others, etc. Just as this Catholic schoolgirl feared getting picked for a profession she didn't want, so might we fear emotions we don't want. Once you get picked, there's nothing you can do but acquiesce.

Increasingly in the twentieth century, we came to assert that the emotions and passions fell within our dominion. This paradigm has ruled the intellectual landscape for the last century or so. Far from poor ships on the sea, blown about defenselessly by the winds of passion, we can and must fight the emotions (or the call to be a nun, etc.). This is the new paradigm. But too few people are willing to discuss the implications of the post-Enlightenment view of improvability. Recent developments in biology threaten this new view and seem to lead us back to the one it supplanted.

We have discovered more about our genes and the chemicals that make our bodies work than we ever knew before. Depression and alcoholism, for example, are no longer personal faults (for the most part). They are now seen as unfortunate conditions some chemically unlucky people must endure. Homosexuality has made enormous ethical inroads because of the increasingly powerful argument that some people are simply "born that way." A Roman Catholic priest jailed for sexually molesting young boys in his parish struggled to change his emotions:

He went regularly to therapy, at first expecting to be told precisely how he could fix his problem. He discovered instead that he would never be cured, that he is a true pedophile. His desire would never leave him. It was like alcoholism, he learned: the disease didn't disappear, but could be controlled. He taught him-

self to look away from attractive adolescent boys he saw on the
street and to bring friends from his support group with him
whenever he had to go places where there were likely to be many
young boys. He learned not to be ashamed of what he felt, but to
take responsibility for what he did with it.[4]

Not blaming someone for being what he is differs from con-
gratulating him. Pedophiles will never find themselves con-
gratulated, not even if they resist their urges until death. The
happiest end to which their self-control can lead is the joy of
relief, relief at having saved children and at having avoided
criminal punishment.

Three thousand years ago, the pre-Socratic philosopher
Heraclitus insisted that character is destiny; we moderns might
protest that biology is destiny, tied as it is to both good and bad
attributes. But aren't we using the words "character" and "biology" in similar ways? Many a religious celibate or religious
ascetic has striven to rise above the sexual desire wrought by a
whirlpool of hormones. The spirit is willing, but the body is
weak. We can no more change some of our instincts than we
can our height or the color of our skin. The popularity of so-
ciobiology, a fusion of Darwinian thinking about evolution
and social theory, has led to the view that just as our genes are
ruthlessly selfish in their quest to survive, so are human beings
in their interactions with others. One obvious problem with
this way of thinking is that genes possess no consciousness and
so cannot represent to themselves selfish drives or choices. And
yet sociobiologists believe they have, once and for all, discovered what we human beings are "really like" deep down inside.

Certainly much is decided by our biology. Kay Redfield
Jamison, an expert on the psychology of suicide, attributes
great power to genes, which she says largely determine our
temperaments, which in turn influence our choices about
which environments we seek out or avoid. Our temperaments
also mold how we respond to our environments and how we
are shaped by them. For those who are low-key and stable, a

disappointment or rejection, the loss of a job or the end of a marriage, or an extended bout of depression will be painful and distressing but not life-threatening. For those with "impulse-laden wiring," life's setbacks and illnesses are more dangerous. For them, it is as though the nervous system had been soaked in kerosene: A fight with a lover, a gambling loss or a run-in with the law, or an irritable flash from a mental illness can ignite a suicidal response.[5]

A growing number of writers and best-selling books focus on our powerlessness in the face of depression. Absorbing key insights of Freud, various psychotherapists have probed how intoxication transcends the ordinary limits of the self and thereby provides a feeling of triumph over depression. Drugs like alcohol, morphine, and heroin work to make you think you've dissolved the usual boundaries around or limitations on yourself. Various forms of bingeing—eating, spending, sex—can provide this same sense of expansion that psychologists call "oceanic bliss." Such ecstasy can also be achieved in love addiction, where the love object is felt to be god-like and thus fusion with that person brings rapture. In such cases, one projects omnipotence, or divine abundance, onto another person and then depends on that person to validate one's own worth. Engaging in such a fantasy is to some degree a universal and celebrated part of falling in love, but the love addict falls in love with the intensity of infatuation itself. Romance soothes disavowed or unacknowledged pain; romance may have nothing to do with the traditional goals of marriage or relationship building.

A difficult question has riven psychiatry: Are mental illnesses like schizophrenia, depression, and personality disorders a matter of biological dysfunction and thus best treated pharmacologically, or are they the product of psychosocial factors—family dynamics, early childhood experiences, the whole closet of Freudian baggage—and thus best treated by psychotherapy? Psychiatrists today still argue over just how much control over our emotions we really wield.

The point of talking about biology in the context of self-control is to demonstrate what a mitigating role biology plays in moral evaluation. For centuries the Roman Catholic Church has held that suicide is a mortal sin. But if we can't help being suicidal, it hardly seems fair to hold us accountable for the mortal sin. Relevant to this point is an adoption study conducted in Copenhagen between 1924 and 1947. If there is a significant genetic influence on suicide, one would expect a much higher rate of suicide in the biological parents of adoptees who commit suicide than in the adoptive parents. This is exactly what was found in Denmark, a country that for years has maintained excellent and comprehensive medical records. An extensive examination of the causes of death in biological relatives established that twelve of the biological relatives of the adoptees who committed suicide had also committed suicide; only two of the biological relatives of the adoptees who had not committed suicide had killed themselves (this was a highly significant statistical difference). None of the adopting relatives of either the suicide or control group committed suicide.[6]

The lesson to be taken from the Denmark adoption study is that we often destroy ourselves because of chemicals in our bodies which subjugate us. The development of drugs that can help to govern and subdue these chemicals would seem to create an ethical responsibility for us to take those drugs. We must keep ourselves from harm, ethically speaking, and if it is our own brain that harms us, then we must declare war on the brain—that is, on that aspect of our brain that is "miswired." Modern psychiatry leaves us with a new version of the mind-body dualism and a newfound sensitivity to the limits of human self-control.

We remain uncertain about the chemical forces within us. *Listening to Prozac* seized the attention of contemporary audiences upon its publication in 1993 and raised the question of whether people gained or lost self-dominion after taking this anti-depressant drug.[7] Psychiatrist Peter Kramer saw the virtue of fighting chemicals (imbalances in the brain) with chemicals. Prozac, he found, can indeed elevate your sense of self-worth and confidence; it can lessen your sensitivity to social rejection, and even enhance your willingness to take risks. He found disconcerting the various cases of depressed patients who took the drug and not only felt better but underwent remarkable personality transformations. Hence the question of whether the medicated or unmedicated version was the person's "real" self.

Think also of cortisol, the chemical borne of stress. In addition to depression, many of us are thinking and talking about stress these days. In stress our brains produce cortisol, a chemical capable of dulling our mental capacities. Frightening or unpleasant possibilities can unleash a liquid that hinders our immune system, in addition to slowing our mental acuity. Now that we know about cortisol, it would seem, we must fight it.

Stress is caused by the outside world, by an impending exam, a recent bereavement, something frightening in the newspaper, or the unremitting exhaustion of caring for a person with Alzheimer's disease. What is most interesting about the recent scientific understanding of cortisol is the way it leaves us with a rosier picture of self-control. Plenty of people think that we are at the mercy of our genes and bodies. Matt Ridley writes persuasively that far from behavior being at the mercy of our biology, our biology is often at the mercy of our behavior.[8] It is the body that switches on genes when it needs them, often in response to a more or less cerebral, or even conscious, reaction to external events. You can raise your cortisol levels just by thinking about stressful eventualities—even fictional ones. Likewise, the dispute between those who believe that a certain suffering is purely psychiatric and those who insist it has a physical cause—consider chronic fatigue syndrome—misses the point entirely. The brain and the body are part of the same system. If the brain, responding to psychological stress, stimulates the release of cortisol and cortisol suppresses the reactivity of the immune system, then a dormant viral infection may well flare up, or a new one catch hold. The symptoms may indeed be physical and the causes psychological. If a disease affects the brain and alters the mood, the causes may be physical and the symptoms psychological.

Focusing on our biological component exerts a dramatic effect on our understanding of our mental or spiritual capacities and has a profound effect on our beliefs about self-control. Although we are still waiting to see, it may just turn out that our minds still prevail over our bodies—despite some medical theories to the contrary. But to the extent that we are also created by forces beyond our control, we cannot be blamed for lapses of self-control.

Our self-control occasionally buckles under the weight of stress management. The struggle affects us differently, leading sometimes to obsessive-compulsive disorders. Although obsessive-compulsive patients represent only one percent of the population undergoing treatment in psychiatric centers, a door-to-door survey identified nearly two percent of Americans as obsessive-compulsive. They are a disturbing group of people to be around, especially in the early phases of the disease, when they still admit to the irrationality of their obsession but seem helpless to do anything about it. David Sedaris's short story "A Place of Tics" from his collection *Naked* introduces us to a boy who has lost control and knows it. He cannot resist lowering his nose to the desk at school, leaving his chair repeatedly, touching his tongue to the classroom light switch, and counting his every step. He explains what an ordinary trip home might look like to someone with OCD:

> It was a short distance from the school to our rented house, no more than six hundred and thirty-seven steps, and on a good day I could make the trip in an hour, pausing every few feet to tongue a mailbox or touch whichever single leaf or blade of grass demanded my attention. If I were to lose count of my steps, I'd have to return to the school and begin again. "Back so soon?" the janitor would ask. "You just can't get enough of this place, can you?"

He had it all wrong. I wanted to be at home more than anything, it was getting there that was the problem. I might touch the telephone pole at step three hundred and fourteen and then, fifteen paces later, worry that I hadn't touched it in exactly the right spot. It needed to be touched again. I'd let my mind wander for one brief moment and then doubt had set in, causing me to question not just the telephone pole but also the lawn ornament back at step two hundred and nineteen. I'd have to go back and lick that concrete mushroom one more time, hoping its guardian wouldn't once again rush from her house shouting, "Get your face out of my toadstool!" It might be raining or maybe I had to go to the bathroom, but running home was not an option. This was a long and complicated process that demanded an oppressive attention to detail. It wasn't that I enjoyed pressing my nose against the scalding hood of a parked car—pleasure had nothing to do with it. A person had to do these things because nothing was worse than the anguish of not doing them.

Bypass that mailbox and my brain would never for one moment let me forget it.[9]

Hilarious and off-putting at the same time, the vivid description of a child who cannot control his own orders should give pause to hard-liners who want to insist that old-fashioned willpower can see us through any personal struggle.

Biochemical determinants of behavior can also cause depression, the common cold of mental health. Psychiatrists report that at any given time, as much as twenty percent of the population suffers from depression, however mild. Andrew Solomon has written one of the frankest and most bracing accounts of the experience of depression to date. Solomon, too, writes of someone who has lost control, and who knows he has lost control.[10] "If you trip or slip, there is a moment, before your hand shoots out to break your fall, when you feel the earth rushing up at you and you cannot help yourself—a passing, fraction-of-a-second horror. I felt that way hour after hour." His courageous narrative of incontinence in public, fear of using the shower in his own apartment, and inability to write make clear that he did not enjoy losing control. No depressed person does.

We are still wrestling with the questions of how far we can blame our genes for our unhappiness. Scientists tell us that I.Q. is fifty percent heritable individually. Whether we will be deaf, alcoholic, or depressed does seem to hinge to some extent on our parents. This means that luck will have a lot to do with morality: Some of us will suffer less than others. Some of us will have a much harder time maintaining self-control, and so the idea that we really do control our emotions (and moods and behaviors) is starting to founder. Luck (or perhaps biology) plays a leading role in the drama of self-control.

Unwanted Thoughts

Joan of Arc, patron saint of France, has inspired more books than practically any other woman through the centuries. She initially came to fame because of the voices she heard in her head, instructing her to save France. Some contemporaries thought the young girl was crazy; others thought she was God's messenger. At first her stray thoughts worked well for her, but eventually they proved to be her undoing (she was put to death because her captors insisted God spoke Latin, not the French she claimed to have heard).

Self-control extends to the mind. Few people will deny that ideas or sayings will just pop into our minds without our inviting them. We must constantly beware of stray thoughts, many of our moralists have concurred (largely for sexual reasons). In his *Confessions*, Augustine mentions a thought that crossed his mind while in church one day; having told us that he judged the thought properly punishable by death, we can guess that it was sexual. Rousseau admits in his own *Confessions* that he once incriminated a woman (on whom he perhaps had a crush) simply because her name, Marion, came into his mind when an authority demanded an explanation of him. Nervous that his theft of a ribbon had been discovered, he found only Marion's name in his head when asked to identify the culprit. He stole, he lied, he accused her without meaning to do so. Writing forty years after the event, Rousseau is still stricken by remorse. Marion was fired without references and very possibly forced into a life of disgrace.

A sad fate also awaited many European women who gave birth to mentally retarded or physically deformed children. In her book *Monstrous Imagination,* Marie-Hélène Huet uncovers medical manuals and social tracts explaining the view (which lasted well into the eighteenth century) that mothers were to blame for the physical imperfections of their infants.[11] It seems that quite a few doctors and philosophers believed impure (and, given the consequences, presumably unwanted) thoughts would manifest themselves in birth defects. Mothers were scorned for having obviously failed to purify their thoughts.

Young children in religious families are taught that God listens carefully to their prayers and expects earnest application to the task. The mental effort necessary for communicating with God requires considerable concentration. Failing at the task can bring on real anxiety.

Daydreams, during which the mind seems to wander aimlessly, differ from intrusive thoughts. It can be frightening, confusing, and dizzying to listen to the thoughts that just pop up in our minds. We wonder where they came from and if we are to blame for them. Schopenhauer introduced us to the notion of unconscious willing in his magnum opus *The World as Will and Representation* (1847). Nietzsche elaborated on Schopenhauer's theories and then Freud reached the formulation of the unconscious that college students still memorize today: superego, ego, and id.

Freud considered the ability to exclude unwanted negative thoughts from conscious awareness a hallmark of mental health. This is accomplished unconsciously (through repression) and consciously (through suppression).[12] Throughout the twentieth century it was said that Victorian women were encouraged to put up with the nuisance of a husband's libido: "Close your eyes and think of England." (Fortunately, Peter Gay has done much to alter our smug assumptions about the Victorians.) Former secretary of education William J. Bennett raised a genuinely insightful objection to TV talk shows ("trash TV"): "This is the world turned upside down. We've forgotten that civilization depends on keeping some of this stuff under wraps."[13] If we could expand on Bennett's position we might find that the problem extends to pulp fiction and yellow journalism as well: There are certain things we are better off not thinking about. Ignorance can prevent us from dangerous experimentation. It's bad enough when unwanted thoughts arise from within our own subconscious; it's unpardonable when the modern media put them there.

Harvard psychologist Dan Wegner has written persuasively that we have little power to fight unwanted thoughts. He concluded that attempts to control our thoughts usually fail for an ironic reason. In order to prevent ourselves from thinking about say, sex, we tend to monitor our thoughts in a way that undermines that control. In order to avoid a thought, we invent a prison guard of sorts who is always on the lookout for that thought. But to keep that prison guard in business, we must regularly remind him or her of the job at hand.

To demonstrate this irony, Wegner focused on a problem he found in Tolstoy's biography. At one time, Tolstoy's older brother had instructed Tolstoy to stand in a corner until he managed to stop thinking about a white bear. Tolstoy had not been thinking of a white bear prior to this challenge but found he could not stop thinking about the white bear while in the corner.

Wegner asked students to say aloud every thought that came into their heads over the course of five minutes, but not to think about a white bear during that time.[14] Student after student failed to keep the white bear out of his or her mind. When these students were later permitted to think about whatever they liked, they reported many thoughts about white bears—even more thoughts about white bears than another group of students, who had been instructed to try to focus on white bears while they said aloud every thought that came into their heads over the course of five minutes.

Wegner's findings help us understand the anxiety of medieval Roman Catholic priests who heard confessions. Helping the faithful examine their conscience required asking them certain leading questions. This was particularly problematic in the case of sexual sins. Priests faced the daunting task of ascertaining just what a man or woman had done wrong without putting ideas into their head, ideas about sexual positions or exploits that might not have occurred to the faithful previously. The Church understood that trying to avoid thinking about something as exciting as sex was like trying to make a stream flow backwards.

The difficulty of controlling our own thoughts shows up regularly in fiction, sometimes to dramatic effect. Earlier we mentioned Buñuel's memorable *Belle de Jour,* one of the cinematic masterpieces of the twentieth century, a film linking the swinging sixties to surrealism. In the film we follow Séverine, a beautiful, recently married Parisian (Catholic, bourgeois) on her day-to-day adventures. Her husband is perfect—handsome, loving, gentle, monied, well bred, a doctor! But there's a problem. Though Séverine cannot stomach the idea of real sex, her dreams and daydreams return her again and again to sexually dangerous fantasies. Fascinated by prostitutes, Séverine eventually becomes one herself, in the distant hope of preparing herself for sex with the princely husband who waits patiently for the moment when his young wife will finally submit to him. Her double life leads Séverine to a tragicomic end. The husband is made an invalid and she becomes, not regretfully, his nursemaid. The dreams have taken over.

In his engrossing novel *In Search of Lost Time,* Proust

ponders involuntary memory, a close relative of unwanted thoughts. In every instance of involuntary memory, from the madeleine through the paving stone, Marcel tries at least briefly to find an explanation of the phenomenon. Proust masterfully shows us again and again how memories come upon us. After an exhausting five-hour train ride, the narrator in "Sodom and Gomorrah" suddenly remembers a time when his grandmother had helped him untie his shoelaces: "I now recaptured the living reality in a complete and involuntary memory."[15] In "Swann in Love," the narrator suggests that Swann's failure as a writer stems at least in part from Swann's addiction to friendship and frivolity and especially to "idolatry," by which Proust means the collector's love of "fine furnishing, beautiful mistresses, and great paintings—the perishable things of this world—rather than the immortal ideas that lie behind them, which can be recaptured only through involuntary memory—and which only then can be codified in great works of literary art." White notes that Proust asserted "only the sudden, unprompted awakenings of memory, triggered by something illogical and unforeseen (the madeleine, for example), could invoke the past in its entirety."

The most condensed explanation of involuntary memory can be found in a scene where the process fails to occur. Late in the book Marcel revisits Combray, where he might expect a torrent of reminiscences. He is disappointed.

> I found the Vivonne narrow and ugly along the towpath. Not that I noticed particularly great inaccuracies in what I remembered. But, separated by a whole lifetime from places I now happened to pass through again, there did not exist between them and me that contiguity out of which is born, before one even notices it, the immediate, delicious, and total flaming up of memory.[16]

These moments occur completely by chance, cannot therefore be chosen or willed, and leave Marcel the mere passive beneficiary of so significant a phenomenon. As Marcel states explicitly many times, he found precedent and confirmation for his experiences of memory in a number of his favorite authors: Nerval, Chateaubriand, Baudelaire, George Eliot, Ruskin. Each of them depicts a particular mode and mood by which the present dovetails with the past.

Involuntary memory might seem to parallel involuntary emotions, about which I have noted some debate between scholars. In any event, involuntary memory would seem to stand in contrast to daydreams, to which we happily give in. Daydreams do not force themselves on us, although preludes to them may lazily turn up in our minds. In an essay from 1908, "Creative Writers and Day-Dreaming," Freud tied artistic creativity both to childhood play and to the temptation to indulge in fantasies or daydreams. Freud believed that "the motive forces of phantasies are unsatisfied wishes, and every single phantasy is the fulfillment of a wish, a correction of unsatisfying reality."[17] If this is so, as I suspect it is, daydreams will be altogether more pleasant than involuntary memories. Still, daydreams can incur the disapproval of moralists, for momentarily "checking out" supposedly amounts to wasting a precious resource, squandering the opportunity to be, to have, to savor a self.

Aside from the obvious fact that daydreams make life more bearable, more interesting, it is also no doubt true that we come to know ourselves better through them. Our deepest desires, our grandest goals, our pettiest faults come into focus. Jerome Singer has fastened on a practical consequence of daydreams in adolescents:

> The adolescent who cannot provide himself pleasure through internal fantasy, contemplation or manipulation of daydream images is compelled more directly to an overt imitation of the adult pattern. He undoubtedly has sexual fantasies at times, but he may be ashamed of these on grounds of various cultural or early family experience; or—and this point has largely been neglected—lacking experience in fantasy play, he may be unable to

expand his fleeting images enough to make them really interesting. Even masturbation, which clearly should provide specific pleasure, may appear less satisfying to an adolescent who lacks the capacity to elaborate imaginatively on romantic situations and sexual partners.[18]

This advantage may be extended to office workers everywhere, all of them now vulnerable on some level to charges of sexual harassment. Beyond that, it must surely be true that the capacity for imaginative exploration enriches our existence.

Unwanted thoughts, though, do not always spice up our days in welcome ways. To the contrary, they land in front of our faces, it sometimes seems, and prevent us from doing what we want. We worry about failing, about not getting done what we should. We fear robbery or physical assault. We dread arguments or betrayals, perhaps ending up alone and lachrymose. We envision an accident befalling someone we love, we try to push out of our minds the calorie counter inside our heads. We wrestle with the persistent image of a humiliating incident that happened years ago. We fight against our own minds. We struggle to change the channel of the radio in our heads as we rue the adventures unwanted thoughts are preventing us from having.

To control our thoughts takes work. To gain the respect of others, to earn and retain a good reputation in the workplace, we need to learn to focus, to drive from our minds unwanted thoughts. Every now and then, though, this goal will strike us as easier said than done. Our best efforts at repression and suppression will only land us right back where we started, daydreaming, fantasizing, and worrying.

New discoveries about the mind raise fresh doubts about who's really in control.

WHEN WE THINK ABOUT MISBEHAVIOR OR PERSONAL problems, it is extremely useful to hold apart two separate threads—what we can control and what we can't. What interests me is the pleasure of giving in to temptation, yielding to what we could control, to letting go of ourselves voluntarily. All that lies beyond our control contrasts with and stands apart from raving, a way of coming to understand ourselves that I address in Part Three. As before, I'll focus on what we're not supposed to do to ourselves.

part three

Raving

Self-Harm

THESE SUB-CATEGORIES ARE NOT EXHAUSTIVE

Stupidity	Self-indulgence	Self-sabotage
IMMEDIATE GRATIFICATION; "CRUISING FOR A BRUISING"	GOAL IS SELF-SATISFACTION; MAKING LIFE A LITTLE EASIER	GOAL IS SELF-DEMOTION; MAKING LIFE HARDER
smoking in a refinery	"night out"	illegal drugs
biting the hand that feeds you	"speaking out"	cutting/burning
insulting a dictator	masturbation	hunger strike
swmming alone	visiting a prostitute	unsafe sex
escaping jail	thrill-seeking	picking nose in interview
spitting in wind	envying/resenting	falling on your sword
burning your bridges	daydreams/fantasies	learned helplessness
not saving for retirement	pornography	predicting your failure

Raving ⟶

THE QUESTION TO WHICH RAVING IS THE ANSWER: *How can we explain individuals who do not seem to take care of themselves?*

Raving hovers over the middle category – self-indulgence. But reasonable people will argue over how to classify what lands in the categories "self-indulgence" and "self-sabotage." And so raving defies easy classification. This makes raving more interesting and more dangerous chapter eight

Raving

==

HOW USEFUL IT IS TO HAVE A WAY TO SUMMARIZE THE many ways in which we transgressively seize control of ourselves! This is what we mean by the word "rave." The rebellious dancers flocking to "raves" illustrate what we ourselves do throughout our lives: We thrill to the power we think we might hide within. These dancers haven't exactly discovered something new: They just taste for themselves the sweet naughtiness ancient Greeks associated with Dionysus, the god of wine.

And What Do We Already Know?

Raving isn't exactly what it seems. Just as the good guy in a novel will sometimes turn out to be the bad guy in the climactic ending, so raving will turn out to be a surprise. We don't drop our guard completely in raving, only partially. Still, we must beware those unintended consequences. The hankering to test our strength while only half guarded can bite us in the back.

Raving, an old and imprecise word, offers a convenient way of summing up what's bad for us. The OED says it may be from Old French *raver,* a variant of *rêver:* to dream, to be delirious. That usage, "to be mad or delirious," shows up as a verb in Chaucer. "To be in a frenzy or show great excitement" dates from the mid-sixteenth century and is first used to describe the fury of winds and waves. Shakespeare uses it to mean "a disordered mental state," and a little later it comes to mean "to talk with enthusiasm or poetic rapture." The word *raving* offers itself as a convenient way of denoting disputed self-harm. Language doesn't bring meaning into existence; conventions bring new words and phrases into language, showing us something we hadn't entirely noticed or, at times, something entirely new.

At times, we marvel that certain words exist at all. After the heated presidential election of 2000, many Americans learned the word "chad," as in the "hanging chads" of Florida. The little circles of paper that pop out of a ballot as it is being punched took on surreal importance. At other times, we coin new words to describe an emerging phenomenon. Posttraumatic stress disorder didn't officially exist until 1980; by 2003, psychiatrists had diagnosed about 8 percent of American adults as suffering from it. Psychological damage from war experience now benefits from a name of its own, a name that sets it off from, say, childhood trauma. In June 2003, the *New York Times* Style section ran a piece on "metrosexuals," heterosexual men who may appear to be homosexual. This piece noted, as had British cultural critic Mark Simpson in 1994, when he coined the term, that more and more men take care of their physical appearance and mind their wardrobe. This new word compels us to ponder whether the pressure to look good has now spanned the gender gap.

At still other times we discover unfamiliar words that suit our present needs just fine. The conceptual artist Matthew Barney began mounting international exhibitions in the 1990s under the title "Cremaster," which is an old and, until Barney's work, virtually unknown word for the muscle governing the raising and lowering of testicles. Barney coopted an existing word in a new and arguably capricious way (his exhibits and films actually focus, the artist has said, on the moment before the sex of a fetus is determined by the chromosomes). I could be accused of the same charge, although I see myself rounding up circulating meanings of the word *raving* in a straightforward way, a way that will be useful to people talking about transgression.

Life unleashes waves of raving and regretting. Adults going off the rails are not always heading for their own destruction: Where do they go and what do they learn? Raving can teach us that.

People who rave seem to have lost a sense of proportion. They have taken leave of their senses, they do not act or behave as they should. When we say that someone has gone "stark, raving mad," we indicate that his or her imagination has trespassed a border we respect. That person has lost a grip on reality. Swooning over rock stars or romance novels, like giving into a temptation to finagle a tax return or play hooky from work, undermines our responsible reputation. Raving helps define rationality as its contrasting idea and experience. The net result of raving benefits both us and them: We develop toleration for, maybe even appreciation of, the quirky imperfections of others. And we find hope to continue on the moral high road while taking a few chances of our own.

Raving is not an argument against virtue, no more than suffering is an argument against life. The fact that you are suffering does not give you sufficient reason to end your life; the fact that you are raving does not give you cause to damn yourself as reprobate.

In Search of a Family Resemblance

The first step to finding our true selves would appear to entail throwing off self-control. Surely the rules we must obey only obstruct search. Besides, rebellion can feel so good. The yearning for escape, to be overwhelmed or defeated by sublimity, threatens our reputations as sensible citizens now, as it did before. In wish-fulfillment, we abandon a dreary existence, the humdrum world we share with our neighbors. Misery loves company, though, and others will sometimes resent our vacations from day-to-day life. They have to maintain self-control, and so we do too.

Common to most examples of willful, sensual risk-taking is the private titillation of raving. Rebellious dancing in contemporary techno-clubs appropriates the word "rave" aptly. Since at least the legendary dances of the bacchantes, certain kinds of dances and ceremonies surrounding those dances have given the appearance of frenzy, of wild abandon. Raving as an intentional leap into rebellion, as the tingle of deliberate defiance, underlies many explanations we hear of why someone ever does something bad for us. Raving suggests a cavalier attitude toward caution, toward the conviction that, in possibly dangerous circumstances, the life you save may be your own. Whereas caution would try to pin uncertainly down, to fix it where we can evaluate it, raving would hurl it into the air and try to keep it there. Those who rave tease the morally serious and throw into question once more the wisdom of playing it safe.

Daydreams and reveries beckon us because we yearn to break free of our confines, or perhaps from the company of others: If we could just own a different life, perhaps a celebrity's, we would taste real happiness! The psychological release of masquerades captivated some of our forebears: They donned costumes and exuberantly wandered rooms full of masked strangers. Costume balls live on in modern-day drag shows and Halloween parties, and crowds still throng to cities such as Venice, New Orleans, and Rio de Janeiro every Mardi Gras to taste the excitement that disguises can ignite. People under thirty flock to parties called "raves," where they writhe to the pulsating beat and deafening tones of electronic music. What's old is new again.

Think here of a new, distinctly personal way of battling institutions that emerged in the twentieth century: the hunger strike. We hold ourselves hostage in order to get what we want from the world. We threaten to harm ourselves and, in doing so, alarm others who expect us to swear off any abuse of our autonomy. Legally, they can't really stop us from hunger strikes.[1] And so they use the word "raving" to describe our troubling attitude and resentfully watch to see how far we'll go. Dancing defiantly, starving defiantly: We use ourselves dangerously.

In the United States, various states have authorized the force-feeding of inmates on hunger strikes. In September 2002, a Livingston County (Illinois) circuit judge ruled that two inmates at a maximum security prison in Pontiac could legally starve themselves, rather than face years of solitary confinement. The two inmates, one convicted of armed violence and the other of rape, then ended their hunger strike. Earlier that same year, doctors at the United States Naval Station at Guantanamo Bay, Cuba began force-feeding two prisoners from Afghanistan who had refused to eat for nearly a month. Joint Task Force 160, the military unit that runs the detention camp, issued a statement, "We give detainees the flexibility to choose to eat or not to eat, but when they refuse meals to a point where they could jeopardize their own lives, we are obligated, as a nation committed to the humane treatment of any human being, to intervene."[2] This creates a Catch-22, in so far as self-starving prisoners are forcibly rehabilitated so that they can be subjected to the same dreary circumstances that led them to choose starvation in the first place. In order to force-feed the prisoners, doctors first sedated them and then inserted a tube through their noses and down their throats.

In the race for novel ways to alarm a government, an Iranian showed unusual creativity in 2003. Abas Amini arrived in Britain after having spent six years in Iranian jails and enduring physical torture. This asylum-seeker went so far as to sew up his eyes, mouth, and ears, then refuse to eat or drink, all in order to protest British immigration authorities, who had opposed his asylum application.[3]

Hunger strikes in turn dovetail with chaperoning. Adults watch children carefully, especially adolescents, whom they regularly try to infect with worry. In the mid-1940s, classroom films became a rite of passage in American high schools. Mental hygiene courses struck terror in the hearts of teenagers who might even think about driving too fast, drinking alcohol, or going "too far" on dates by showing them lurid reenactments and documentary footage of worst-case scenarios. Today the equivalent films are still shown, now about "safe sex" as well as drinking before driving. They are generally less hysterical than their predecessors. These cautionary tales are the secular translations of religious traditions that reached back centuries.

A history of raving would almost have to include mention of "hysteria," a condition men long imputed to women who didn't behave, and of the "exotic," the intoxicating otherness that many imperialistic Caucasians have felt when confronted with the music, art, or flesh of darker-skinned peoples. And a history of raving would also detail religious fanaticism. Raving can explain Jewish and Christian understandings of sin, specifically the mental state in which people transgress divine law and then regret it (or deny God's existence altogether: Believers and atheists may see each other as raving).

Although God presumably always knows when we step out of bounds, often others never do. When celebrities, nobles, or politicians rave, they make news and sometimes change history. In the early 1900s, Nicholas and Alexandra raved: They sacrificed Russia while seeking help for their hemophiliac son. In England, the Duke of Windsor raved: He sacrificed the crown for an American divorcée named Wallace Simpson.

Further examples of public raving will draw nods of recognition from non-celebrities who've taken similar leaps. These examples call out for classification and explanation. In 1992, the popular Irish singer Sinead O'Connor appeared on the American television show "Saturday Night Live" and, to the shock of the show's producers, ripped up a photograph of Pope John Paul II, just after proclaiming, "Fight the real enemy." She was referring to the Pope's continued disapproval of contraception, abortion, and women priests. Two weeks later,

O'Connor appeared in concert with Bob Dylan in New York City and was booed off the stage at Madison Square Garden. And in the summer of 2002, a French national living in Washington, D.C., flipped his lid out of frustration with the new security requirements in American airports. After one of the screeners in Miami asked him to turn his belt over, Marc Danselme, 62, became irate, dropped his pants, and asked, "Is this good enough?" Fellow passengers, as well as some children, were present when Danselme exposed himself, police said. He was arrested and taken to the airport's police station, where he was charged with "prohibited conduct."[4] Regardless of place or time, raving exceeds garden-variety irresponsibility. Raving threatens our commonsense judgment, that which ties us to our social worlds and legal systems.

Raving can naturally embarrass us. University of Virginia lacrosse player John Christmas raved in the national championship game of 2003. The sophomore scored a goal with only two minutes remaining. Elated, he galloped thirty yards off into the field, toward a group of equally jubilant Virginia fans. Referees then pulled Christmas off the field, citing "unsportsmanlike conduct." After the championship, the chastened player told the *Washington Post*: "In a game of this magnitude, the emotion was pumping. It's really hard keeping your composure. I ran because I was so excited, but the referees thought it was too much."[5] Raving usually strikes others as too much.

Flying Solo, in Style

Our age, like ones past, still looks with suspicion on those who turn their backs to the world. As children we learn nursery rhymes such as "The Farmer in the Dell" and "Boys and Girls, Come Out to Play" that impart a healthy desire to live in communities. Even as teachers and parents explain the importance of self-reliance, they hasten to insist that no man is an island. We wince at the thought of being sent off to solitary confinement in a prison. As adults, we sing the praises of constructing communities and undertaking public service. Although we argue over government, we shudder at the idea of anarchy. We affirm that there is something wrong with retreating into ourselves and point out that even religious groups devoted to prayer will structure worship around social rituals and rhythms. How interesting that in the new age of technology, artists and intellectuals, many of them long exiled to the margins of society as irrelevant, are now jumping at the chance to appear on television talk shows and op-ed pages. How disconcerting that the Internet police get better and better at listening in on us when we had hoped we were alone. Solitude is out.

"Cool," however, is in. A very many people, not all of them under the age of thirty and not all of them inhabitants of English-speaking countries, yearn to embody what the advertising industry struggles to keep its finger on: coolness. Cool reflects excellent, up-to-the-minute self-regulation. Through cool, teenagers and others defy authority. And so those who self-identify as cool, in part through using the word "cool," differ from many of our forebears, who consciously strove to please a father figure (for example, God, the king, or one's actual father). African-American leaders, eager to explain the discrepancy between standardized test scores between children of different racial groups, insist that part of the problem has something to do with kids trying to be cool. Many teenagers grow up thinking that scholastic achievement just isn't cool and so don't exert much effort on studies. It's not that adolescents of color lack self-control, just that they resist cultural currents which would engage their minds in a certain way. Raving, to the extent that it plays off of provocation of authority, is cool. Although weak performances in academic endeavors don't count as raving, the very idea of deliberately defying the standards of a powerful group requires the same understanding of resisting social control that defines raving.

Critics argue over the provenance of cool, and landing upon the answer could certainly help describe the goals of cool. But no matter: It is safe to say that cool signifies nonchalance in the face of one's duties to social superiors. The ironic detachment underneath the cool demeanor challenges traditional hierarchies and values. Much more remains to be said about this, to be sure, but it is enough to note here that by the late twentieth century, post–World War II, post-Watergate and Vietnam, post–Iron Curtain and the USSR, obedience to parents and affirmations of a personal relationship with God became profoundly uncool in most of Europe and the English-speaking world. To be cool was to aspire to belong in a group united by opposition to authority, even though codes of cool quickly took on an authority of their own.

An older generation may openly resent a younger cohort's reverence for a newer notion of cool. And our neighbors may straightforwardly disapprove of our madness and our ecstasy, either one of which can be confused with raving or being cool. In raving, we fail to govern ourselves as they wish. In cool, we similarly disdain their wishes by putting ourselves above them, by deliberately standing apart from them.

Thinking about raving helps us to understand how we evaluate people around us and how we internalize moral lessons from them. What is interesting is disagreement, for when we rave we often believe that we are seizing the day, putting fear and timidity behind us, and tasting independence. When we rave, we may insist that *they* are the irrational ones.

In any event, raving exposes a gulf between us and them. Negotiating that gulf may sometimes seem a necessary step to self-fulfillment. Raving revolves around self-fulfillment and compels us to ask whether we have to step outside ourselves in order to become who we really are. If our own raving is in question, we will likely reply that we are stepping outside of social conventions. As for the raving of someone we like, we may either applaud or simply shake our heads in exasperation and conclude that she is just not herself. The raving of someone we dislike or fear will put us on guard.

Raving also leads us away from the pack, perhaps even into

solitude. This is a problem. Psychoanalysis tells us that human happiness grows out of group identity. Philosophers such as Kant tell us that we have an ethical duty to join a community. With the exception of the odd genius, we humans generally want to run with a pack.

If it is true that we want to live in community, it is also true that we want to live autonomously. The delicious but dizzying freedom in raving can tell us something important about our commitment to personal autonomy; this freedom outlines our ideal of the moral life. If we cannot rave, then we cannot challenge our communities; nor can we enjoy robust freedom of expression. This is not to say that there is no such thing as irrationality or even insanity, only to question who gets to define irrationality and insanity.

Raving lies in the eye of the beholder.

Danger Ahead

Raving captures two kinds of danger—madness and transgression. Going "stark, raving mad" won't appeal to anyone, but being swept away by romance will. Between these two kinds of trespass lies much of what makes our lives interesting. Consider the second kind of danger, falling in love. Invested as it is with risk (that our love may not be reciprocated, or that any subsequent sexual activity may defy religious rules or lead to venereal disease), falling in love in spite of ourselves may resemble the feeling brought on by contemplating wrongdoing. When we fall in love, we give up some large measure of control over ourselves. Whether our love proceeds tragically or comically or somewhere in between is not a foregone conclusion. *Othello* or *Twelfth Night*? *Antony and Cleopatra* or *A Midsummer Night's Dream*?

When we stray, we sometimes find it difficult to block out the voice of conscience. We have to respond somehow, and so we say something like, "What I'm doing now isn't really so bad" or "What I'm doing now doesn't count as an offense because of when/where/how I'm doing it." Just as someone on a diet may tell him or herself, "There are no calories in nibbling," so may a transgressor say, "There's no harm in a little overstep under the right circumstances." This is what rationalization is all about. It is difficult to condemn such thinking out of hand, however, for it marks the moral imagination at work, a mind exploring the rules it aims to adopt.

If there weren't more to raving than just danger, we'd never allow ourselves to rave. The joy of raving lifts us out of ordinary existence; a gorgeous pleasure fills us with the sense that now, at last, we have seized life by the horns. The stultifying routine of daily life or oppressive social conventions crumble. Adoring fans rave over rock singers or sports stars; religious followers speak in tongues or swoon over apparitions of the Virgin Mary. When the spiritually unhinged offer their prayers, the enthusiasm sometimes reaches a fever pitch. Regardless of the precipitating activities or contexts, the euphoria of raving unites all who seek it.

Our freedom to express ourselves has not diminished basic moral expectations that our neighbors harbor. Our communities still extol self-control. A momentary loss of self-control (a careless roll in the hay, stepping behind the wheel of a car after a drink too many, saying aloud what we really think) can ruin someone's life. A single loss of self-control can blacken the whole future, because of the alleged likelihood that it will recur. Our integrity suffers after others learn of a lapse in our self-control, and we have to work hard to restore confidence lost. It only takes a minute to undo a lifetime of work.

Not Quite the Last Straw

Raving stands between good and evil precisely because raving truncates transgression. We travel to a border we genuinely fear and then turn around. We explore the forbidden, but we do not succumb to it. Moreover, we experiment with our-selves—we don't use other people to satisfy our own curiosity.

Raving describes the place where transgression meets self-awareness. It is the moral laboratory in which we isolate rudi-mentary concepts and then hold them up to the light. Anyone who would deny the morality of such tinkering would con-demn raving as simply another manifestation of transgression (according to the Jewish and Christian traditions, death en-tered the world as a result of sin and transgression [Genesis 3:16–19; Romans 5:12]; religious people will naturally take transgression very seriously indeed).

Does transgression somehow honor virtue? Is breaking a rule a perverse way of honoring a rule? Some scholars have tried to explain Satan in just this way: Satan's blasphemy ends up, despite his intentions, paying tribute to God. In the climax of Christopher Marlowe's play *Doctor Faustus* (c. 1588), for ex-ample, Faustus, who has made a deal with the devil, calls upon Christ to save his soul. Imploring God's mercy despite having blasphemed earlier, Faustus too belatedly glorifies his Savior.

There is something to this idea. Raving wouldn't hold any thrill for us if we didn't care about maintaining self-control. Think of the rules by which other people live: Many of them don't concern us in the least. Orthodox Jews, for example, insist on strict dietary specifications that non-Jews likely never pon-der. I, for example, have never spent any time wondering whether I was debasing myself or offending God by eating non-kosher food. Non-Jews can hardly conceive of themselves as rav-ing while eating non-kosher food because they simply don't think they're transgressing or losing control of themselves.

Augustine locates the origin of transgression in the Fall, the consequence of which was a loss of selfhood for all men. Suffering endures and finds expression in the experience of sin: "The retribution for disobedience is simply disobedience itself. For man's wretchedness is nothing but his own dis-obedience to himself, so that because he would not do what he could, he now wills to do what he cannot" (*City of God,*

XIV.15). Augustine drives home the message that we get to know ourselves better through transgression. In his *Confessions*, for example, he upbraids himself for having stolen pears from an orchard as a young man:

> With the basest companions I walked the streets of Babylon.... Our only pleasure in [theft] was that it was forbidden....The malice of the act was base and I loved it—that is to say I loved my own undoing, I loved the evil in me—not the thing for which I did the evil, simply the evil: my soul was depraved and hurled itself down from security in You into utter destruction, seeking no profit from wickedness but only to be wicked...if I took so much as a bite of any one of those [stolen] pears it was the sin that sweetened it. (II. iii–iv)

Augustine sees himself as having honored God through a guilty conscience. We can extend to raving Augustine's intuition that what pleased him was not what he stole but simply that he stole. It's the feeling of transgression we crave—not so much because we want to break a rule (although sometimes we most certainly do), but because we yearn to feel power. According to Augustine, the improper use of power enslaves us to a bad conscience. Even if we're not found out, bad conscience is the price of raving.

Curbing Urges

Understanding the limits of our self-control raises moral questions: Is raving crudely selfish, or is it a reasonable step toward self-fulfillment? Does raving always involve joy? solitude? visible/audible expression? How does self-expression impinge on the lives of others? What do we owe others? Answers to these questions, answers which vary across continents and within nations, delimit raving.

Self-control covers matters large and small. More important than avoiding sloppy dress and keeping our hair neatly trimmed, we must keep our simmering passions under lid. And we must remain who we are, as opposed to pretending to be someone else. Acting combines both these sins. Rousseau (among many others before and after) asserted that impersonation diminishes the dignity of a person. Actors hurt themselves by playing others.

Curiously, Rousseau also believed that life in big cities harms us. We lose ourselves in the hustle and bustle; we find and hold onto ourselves in small towns. Urban environments slyly corrupt even the best of us, Rousseau observed in the *Letter to M. d'Alembert*. Gradually, they pry loose our grip on self-control. Elsewhere, Rousseau contrasted self-preserving sentiments like fear, anger, curiosity, and shame with species-preserving feelings, like fear and sympathy.[6] Both classes of sentiments contribute to the answer of why certain acts and attitudes are bad for us.

Why have moral thinkers assumed that losing control signifies fault, weakness, or perversion? Just what is so bad about giving up control? Sometimes (as with drunk driving, or "safe sex" in the age of AIDS, or any sex in the age when illegitimate pregnancy was an overriding fear), the answers to these questions are easy to see. But when we decide against cosmetic surgery or a diet sure to reduce our waistlines, the answers may become harder to articulate to others. I see raving as the answer to the question of where our personal freedom begins to end. Raving is all about harming ourselves—from someone else's perspective—and achieving ourselves, from our own.

Religious, artistic, and sexual expression have challenged the limits of moral autonomy as perhaps no other forces have. These experiences, vital to the lives of the vast majority of ancients and moderns alike, perpetuate anxiety over what many have perceived to be a war between reason and the emotions. Philosophers since the time of Socrates have openly worried about the passions, which supposedly undermine reason. This is complicated terrain, for the very commitment to reason or truth can itself become quite emotional. Raving is the way of thinking about emotions urged on us by a culture that distrusts emotions: Raving is the category through which one group of people dominates, restructures, and exercises authority over another.

Raving revolves around exultation and guilt, two disparate emotions. What do the emotions have to do with harm to the self? A lot. Disgust is harm to self as anger is harm to others. Disgust, such as Augustine felt for himself after stealing pears, spurs us to turn our heads away from a situation, to avoid the unpleasant thought or sight. Anger compels us to change conditions that strike us as unjust or unfair. This distinction helps us to see that there are (at least) two ways of asking transgressors, "How could you DO that?" In criminal transgressions (to others), we express anger more than anything else. In moral transgressions (to the self), we express disgust more than anything else. Our emotions prompt and guide our sense of justice, much as they do our sense of beauty. We cannot understand prohibitions on harm to the self without attending to the emotions. Reverence for willpower as the antidote to temptation tends to overlook the varieties of perfectly rational uses to which willpower may be put.

Raving includes rage, a familiar passion. Although anger is unpleasant, expressing anger can be pleasantly satisfying. We might argue over the opposite of anger: is it satisfaction or lethargy? Regardless of disagreement, anger and satisfaction both suffuse us with a vivid sense of being alive. Indifference does not. It is possible to cherish anger. Women and men cope with anger differently; "It is a psychiatric cliché that disturbed men tend to act out their aggression on others and end up in jail, whereas disturbed women tend to act out on themselves— slash their wrists, take overdoses—and end up hospitalized."[7] Women would appear to be bad for themselves in a way that men do not.

Raving stops just short of mental illness. More often than

not raving feels good. We are liable to lose control when we are enjoying ourselves (for example, religious rituals, sex, drugs, alcohol, masturbation, dancing, warfare, gambling, diving into the stock market, climbing mountains, shopping, surfing the Internet, dressing up in costume, satisfying wanderlust). The dazzling variety of forms raving can assume might fill a cumbersome inventory. There is danger in raving: Allowing ourselves to be swept away may land us in prison or an asylum. Toying with nothingness may end in the loss of autonomy, which we may not be able to recover from others. Early American slave traders argued that the Africans they transported to North America had no selves and so deserved no rights. Nazis later made a similar claim about Jews and thereby justified labor camps. These extreme examples remind us of the social worth of a self. Raving puts the self at risk.

Raving brings to light the emotions at work. Begging forgiveness from a priest or someone we've wronged will unleash private tears; a cathartic surrender runs its course almost in secret. Sometimes, as I've said, raving spills over into public expression. Seditious emotions spring up in all of us, and we labor to hide their evidence from neighbors who would disapprove of, say, our failure to feel compassion. Unless, of course, they were feeling it too (think here of Lord Jeffrey Archer's spectacular fall from grace in 2001 or Martha Stewart's in 2002 or Trent Lott's later that same year). Our gleeful or defiant flouting of social conventions (such as proper table manners or keeping our voices down in public spaces) bothers the public quite a bit less than our decision to earn a little extra money through prostitution. Even so, there is a deep connection between morals and manners (the French word *moeurs* can mean both). For over two thousand years, philosophers and religious thinkers have warned us against the emotions, which supposedly weaken our hold on morals. Others use the word "raving" as a weapon in order to douse the fire of our emotions. Raving helps us understand how it is that others justify themselves morally when they tell us to change our ways.

We do not exactly govern our selves, given that the world legally penalizes us for losing ourselves in certain ways (for example, trying to commit suicide) and morally inhibits inner inclinations to self-abandonment (as, for example, in casual sex or drug trips). Contemporary mores in the West disapprove of selves that drift away into solitude. Even, or especially, in the midst of intensely social events, we can find ourselves all alone. This is not raving in most cases, though; rather, it is more likely to be a withdrawal from the raving of others. Raving isolates us from the social world in which we live and learn. Raving contrasts with ways in which we temporarily forget ourselves, such as contemplating works of great art or reading great books. A declining yet still strong presumption against solitude informs moral life in the West. Raving represents a retreat from other people, accompanied by pleasure or at least relief.

A closer look at raving can help us understand the moral basis for denying full autonomy to competent persons (as, for example, in sabotaging a friend's efforts to land a new job or refusing to help a terminally ill person end it all). As we have seen, the OED's definition of raving places extreme expression of emotions in a social context. The raver is over the line of decorum. Because a fundamental assumption about moral agency—that mentally competent people want to maintain self-control—seems wrongheaded, raving amounts to a philosophical problem. Why is it that self-affirmation seems to require self-surveillance and self-overcoming? Conflicting desires confuse us: the yearnings to be free and not free, to be wild and not wild.

Like the Icarus of mythology, many of us yearn to fly. We dream about flying away from personal problems, political catastrophes, natural disasters, poverty, even a comfortable but colorless existence. If we could fly, we would leave behind others who might begrudge us our freedom, our power. If we could fly, we would soar straight into self-fulfillment. Since we cannot fly, we try falling. The contrary feelings resemble one another in raving.

Fear of raving constricts the human sciences, which for the most part assume that individuals want to maintain uninterrupted, full control of their thoughts, feelings, and behavior. "Rational choice" theory makes this assumption explicit: It cascades through moral philosophy as well. As a result, moral philosophy has focused on the surface of conduct, rather than investigating its depths. Experiments and surveys in the human sciences assume that their subjects are aware of their own motives and feelings, and that they say what they mean and mean what they say. In *The Interpretation of Dreams*, Freud took the functioning of dreams as systematic evidence of the unconscious. Since Freud, many psychoanalytic thinkers have seized upon our fantasies and fears and subsequently questioned the full-control assumption. Dreams and fantasies may feed raving, but that is not to say that raving is irrational. In raving, we believe ourselves to be acting rationally.

Raving: Losing Control and Liking It

Sometimes we delight in losing self-control, and sometimes we lament it. We can lose self-control in different ways, as I pointed out in chapter seven (which explains what raving is *not*). We rave on purpose. And although we may appear to others to be harming or even sabotaging ourselves, we feel a heady rush of adrenaline.

Raving amounts to succumbing to ourselves. Desires and impulses oppose beliefs and restraints in Kant's thinking: he exhorts us to favor and cultivate the latter. Kant denies that emotions can overtake us; we allow ourselves to be overtaken by emotions, he insists. In censuring the freedom to "debase" ourselves, Kant depicts raving as an offense against humanity. Note the extent to which morality hangs on keeping humans separate from the animals. The fear of sex in the theology of Augustine and Aquinas comes down to the same thing: anxiety over the distinction between human and animal. This anxiety underlies fundamental assumptions about a moral life.

Kant thought of raving in terms of *Schwärmerei,* a particularly expressive German word that means undisciplined enthusiasm or emotional turbulence. He associated *Schwärmerei,* which he loathed, with Goethe. An enemy of our passions, Kant heralded the salvific power of reason and decried the corrupting influence of emotions, which he maintained only clouded reason.

On the edge of madness, raving hovers over other distinctions, such as that between man and the divine. Artistic creation—whether of music, painting, or literature—might seem impossible without raving (even if we think of creativity as exemplifying the serenely ordered mind, still it remains that many of greatest artists marched to the beat of a different drummer). Falling in love—with God or with a mere mortal —also pries us loose of our senses and carries us off somewhere. Whether we drift toward the angels or slide into madness remains open to debate, but the experience of passionate love turns on raving. In other, socially charged contexts—such as abortion, military service, hunger strikes, physician-assisted suicide, and the insanity defense—our neighbors will argue over our moral fortitude, our personal judgment, our self-control. Whether they determine us strong enough to do the right thing will govern their emotional responses. When we cannot help ourselves, we will likely receive sympathy from somewhat frightened neighbors. When we allegedly violate ourselves out of willfulness or perversity, we will receive anger, scorn, or blame.

Our notion of raving changes from age to age, much in the way I indicated in chapter one. If raving signifies the harm we supposedly do to ourselves, then we should expect the category to evolve, just as our knowledge of harm does. And that is the case. We now understand as we never did before what a genetic predisposition to alcoholism, Alzheimer's, or drug addiction might mean (we have not yet established a genetic predisposition to sexual infidelity). We now understand weakness of the will better, too. We know that a change in diet will help us dramatically, or a change in how we allow ourselves to unwind after a hard week in school or at the office, although we may not have the resolve to follow through on our good intentions. More pointedly, in the modern world we may feel ourselves culturally, as well as economically, compelled to sacrifice the time we might have spent on family, in order to distinguish ourselves professionally. Otherwise, we fear, we will harm our chances to move up the corporate ladder or charge ahead in the work world. Let the Europeans take their six-week holidays; we'll soldier on!

I am not really interested in the question of rights, in arguing for moral permission to do whatever we like with our own persons (even though I sympathize with libertarians). What interests me is how other people justify changing our private behavior. The increasingly corporate nature of society, coupled with studied silence or "correctness" about ethnic, sexual, and political peculiarities, make criticism of others more awkward than ever. Raving now describes what we object to in others but cannot bring ourselves to condemn. Recourse to this description—"He raved about this" or "She went stark, raving mad"—will happen more and more often in a world with more porous cultural frontiers. Just as in the past it indicated disappointment with someone else's talent for self-regulation, so does it today.

What can we learn from the encounter between transgression and self-knowledge? Understanding how people decide to sin, to blast off into bliss, or to follow the beat of a different drummer can sensitize us to the always urgent matter of human suffering. This understanding can also drive home the difficulty of becoming who it is we really believe ourselves to be.

Intentionally giving up self-control, central as it is to our moral lives, sometimes does less harm than good. Beyond that, there is little compelling reason to think of raving as intrinsically immoral. There have been numerous studies of evil, but I am interested in less dramatic wrongdoing: moral lapses, especially moral relapses on the part of people who claim to be doing the best they can or who insist they are doing nothing wrong. In raving, moral lapses flow into lapses of judgment: We knew that the Botox injection might backfire and leave us looking shell-shocked for six weeks, but we closed our eyes and risked it anyway.

Raving: My Favorite Mistake

Raving will help us to see that being ourselves isn't all that it's cracked up to be. We may be more authentically ourselves when we give in to temptation than when we resist: That's a problem. We are the sum total of our desires, both good and bad. When we swear off what it is that we want in the name of something we want even more (perhaps to be able to call ourselves moral), we split ourselves in two. We say "I could have kicked myself" to indicate our disappointment with the truth about ourselves. Our raving may be authentic, but it is hardly flattering. The whole class of things considered bad for us must represent this nagging struggle within ourselves if we are to feel virtuous about overcoming anything.

In the best and the worst moments of our lives, we rave. Exaggerated emotions, like exaggerated speech, signal that something has gone too far. In raving, we audition for ourselves, trying on a new role for size. Through raving we temporarily lose or overcome ourselves. We risk slipping away to madness, a place to which others lose us permanently. Transcending but not destroying the self, raving illustrates the limits others place on our freedom. In raving, we risk who we are in order to flirt with what we might become. Our raving cheats others of their say in what we do, just as it offers us a breathtaking view of the naked self. Raving casts light on a world at war with its own emotional diversity.

You only live once, we reason before stepping out of line. And a day of pleasure is worth two of sorrow. Even if the world should later make us pay for pleasure, we will have the sweet memory of our escapade. In any event, it is easier to ask for forgiveness than permission to do something we shouldn't. Raving may surface in memory as a favorite mistake.

The problem with manufacturing justifications is that we may have inflicted serious harm to our reputations by the time we feel the sting of regret. We will have run from the menacing realization of our supreme power to spoil the future.

Some Restrictions May Apply

Could the answer to the raving riddle be as simple as "All things in moderation"? No, it's more a matter of "Sometimes you win, sometimes you lose." So, then, let the raver beware. Moderation may still be a good idea, yet mainstream Americans today seem to be fall in line behind Mae West, who once quipped that too much of a good thing is wonderful.

On some level, anything we do could be bad for us. Think of trusting in a friend; that friend could later turn on you and end up hurting you by exploiting the confidence you had shared. Think of stepping into a city street: You just never know when a bicycle or car may come hurtling into you. Even being born presents certain problems: Not being circumcised, for instance, leaves males more likely to suffer from bladder infections, contract HIV, or come down with penile cancer. But being circumcised leaves male infants vulnerable to a knife that might slip. The list of what's bad for us races away from us; I want to focus on what we do to ourselves.

There is such a thing as a "victimless crime," a concept that came into vogue in the 1970s. Smoking, for example, does harm cigarette devotees, even though they may tell us to mind our own business. Those who speak of victimless crimes usually insist that only individuals may judge what's bad for them. Few people will intentionally do themselves in; self-harm wouldn't be very interesting if it weren't for the fact that few of us understand that we're doing ourselves in when we permit self-indulgence.

Raving can confuse us, as we can't always tell whether it is a cause or effect of an emotional state. Internet addiction, for instance, may not be so much bad for us in itself as an indication that something else in our life has gone terribly wrong. Dependence on the Internet shows no measurable physiological effect, yet many dependents may complain of depression or manifest symptoms resembling obsessive-compulsive disorder.

Our compulsively confessional age serves up television programs and bookstore memoirs in which people sob over being swept away. Resuming whatever it was that swept them away then wouldn't necessarily start the fireworks all over again. For it was likely the state of being carried away—at a particular time and place and age, under a particular set of circumstances—that they really relished. The various kinds of naughtiness that create raving pale in comparison to raving itself.

Once a Cheater, Always a Cheater?

According to a popular saying, "Once a cheater, always a cheater." The maxim usually refers to men who have betrayed their wives, not students who have taken an unfair advantage on a test. Unhappy wives listening to a husband's apology walk on broken glass.

Adultery provides a good illustration of how losing self-control creates negative expectations. A perfectly good man who genuinely wishes to be faithful to his wife may fail. He will likely describe his sin of passion as an isolated lapse of self-control. He will swear never to fall again. Will he succeed?

It would be interesting to see a statistical survey of recidivism among contrite adulterers, male and female. It should be possible for an adulterer to reform and to swear off further infidelities. The prevalence of this saying (sometimes applied to tax dodgers as well) suggests popular skepticism, however.

Here is another downside of raving: Once tasted, the fruit might seem irresistible. This stands to reason. The truth of the saying depends to some extent on the logic of a slippery slope—once you take a step off the path of righteousness, you are doomed. That is to say that once you start raving, you will never stop.

I, for my part, am not convinced. What ravers seek is not necessarily the fruit of transgression as the *thrill* or *feeling* of transgression. Of course, sometimes what people who step across the line really want is what lies on the other side of the line.

What difference does this make to the unhappy woman whose husband begs forgiveness? With the answer to why her husband raved, she can better predict future happiness in her marriage. If what he really wants is the sensation of letting go, he can find it in other ways. However, if he falls prey to the charms of other women, she is in trouble. Ann, Abby, and Oprah would tell her as much, too.

Thrill-seekers may proceed from fast cars to illegal drugs to bungee jumping to parachuting out of planes. After a certain point, the thrills become quite dangerous. The challenge of slaking the thirst for euphoria grows as the list of things never tried diminishes. In hindsight, it may well seem preferable never to have tried thrillseeking at all.

The idea that raving feeds on itself and fuels an ever-deepening hunger rests on the assumption that bad habits can't be broken. Such cynicism fails to recognize that many of us do manage to reform ourselves; this cynicism feeds off of a fear of powerlessness, the same powerlessness raving happens to overcome. And so we discover the possibility of inverse raving: leaping over and frustrating the negative expectations of others.

That Achilles Heel

Merchandisers use rebate coupons to lure us into purchases. Why don't merchandisers just give us the rebates up front? They know that many customers will drop the ball and, through carelessness or laziness, fail to file for the rebate. Customers will then have only themselves to blame. We can hardly criticize people running a business for trying to maximize profits. Meanwhile, we insist that no one knows better than we what is good for us. Despite the protestations of close friends, we may marry for money, only to find ourselves miserable and earning every penny our spouse grudgingly throws our way. Yesterday we had our way, and today we have no one to blame but ourselves. (On the other hand, we may make a success of the marriage and drop our doubting friends.)

"Paternalism" has become a dirty word, as what it stands for expresses something repugnant to anyone suspicious of help from above. An individual's basic rights to complete autonomy compete with paternalism continually. Neither undermines the psychological impact of sharing.

Governing our private little world sounds fine and good, but sharing that world with someone else often sounds even better. Sharing pleasures intensifies them; sharing burdens lessens them. Culturally, we hold the pleasures of sex between two people above the pleasures of masturbation. Plenty of people consider it better to take a sightseeing trip to Europe or Asia with another person, no matter how strained our relationship with that person might be. Traveling alone, like dining by yourself, strikes many people as sad. For the majority of people, having someone to share the thrill of seeing Paris from the top of the Eiffel Tower beats taking in the vista alone. The power of sharing extends to suffering as well; you hardly have to be a psychiatrist to understand that depressed friends will feel at least somewhat better if you can induce them to articulate their worries and disappointments. Virtually anyone who has ever suffered will attest that talking makes us feel better.

And so, much as we may insist on personal power over ourselves, we have to admit that what others think or say or do has a lot to do with how happy we will ultimately be. No man is an island.

Not surprisingly, others may believe some of our whims to be disguised cries for help. Take, for example, Munchhausen syndrome, where healthy patients seek medical help, surgery, and sympathy for wounds they inflict upon themselves. It's not that some people will do anything for attention, it's that some people have a hard time asking for help. If you understand that injuries to the body signal one of the surest paths to the sympathy of others and you feel reluctant to simply ask for the sympathy of others, damaging your own body begins to look like a clever idea. Armchair psychologists say that obesity in general or overindulgence in fast food masks a similar cry for help. The list goes on.

Our own rescue fantasies can end up doing us in, though, because not everyone in apparent trouble secretly seeks our intervention. Plenty of kids taking Ritalin or other attention deficit medications complain that they don't feel themselves after having taken medication. Sure, they feel more in control of themselves, but they report feeling like another person, a stranger in their own minds. And so they may resist taking medication, not because they want more attention from us, but because they want to find the way back to themselves.

We like to be thrilled, to perch ourselves on the brink of disaster. We take roller coaster rides and immerse ourselves in murder mysteries and horror stories. We place ourselves in harm's way deliberately, for a variety of sometimes complicated reasons. The right to hurt or help ourselves will trouble those who wish us well. Our friends desire to protect us from ourselves, to educate us, but we see it as a restriction of our freedom. We may not be thinking clearly at any given moment, which means they are right to worry. Or, they may see more clearly than we the dizzying decline to which our liberty is leading.

The wisdom of letting off a little steam every now and then, or marching to the beat of our own drummer generally, includes danger. "Raving," as I have called the planned vacation from the self, recommends itself to those capable of respecting limits. But people with little self-control may, through raving, put themselves on a self-destructive path. What begins as an exercise designed to strengthen resolve may end up as the sword that kills it.

And so, while raving can cure many ills, caution should prevail. Like Icarus flying too close to the sun, we may find ourselves toppling to the earth in raving, with no one to blame but ourselves. What is bad for us? We are bad for us, when all is said and done.

chapter nine

The Whole World's Gone Mad

WHAT'S BAD FOR AN INDIVIDUAL MAY BE BAD FOR A society. Just as an individual can rave, so can a culture. In the early twentieth century, Freud, speaking as a social critic, said that religion was every bit as bad for a culture as it was for the individual. Today, social critics bring to light self-destructive delusions that grip cultures, whether those include ethnic hatred in the former Yugoslavia or in Rwanda, alcoholism in Russia, or causes of terrorism in the Middle East. In this chapter, I am also speaking as a social critic. I will be addressing changes I see as likely to occur in American morals in the near future.

So Happy Together

How can an entire society get swept away? Both fear and hope can create overriding emotional bonds between people of very different backgrounds. Americans have gotten carried away together on numerous occasions: think of the 1849 Gold Rush, the 1920s flappers, the Boston frenzy around the Sacco-Vanzetti trial, the Boise, Idaho, homosexual panic of the late 1950s, the swing to patriotism after 9/11. Getting swept away differs from mass hysteria, which is what happened after Orson Welles's infamous "War of the Worlds" radio broadcast and arguably what plagued the good people of Massachusetts during the Salem Witch Trials.

Social change also happens in carefully thought out, delib-

erate ways. Think here of American civil rights legislation eras-
ing Jim Crow laws in the 1960s. In the same decade, the Second
Vatican Council (1962–65) overrode the spirit and culture of
the First Vatican Council (1869–70), and several religious laws
as well. The droves of Catholic priests and nuns who left the
religious life in the 1970s and 1980s in order to marry and raise
families were not raving, but embracing the suddenly vindicated secular culture.

John McWhorter's provocative book *Losing the Race* ac-
cuses African Americans of sabotaging their own chance for
social advancement by preaching a self-defeating gospel of
victimhood.[1] McWhorter believes his people have allowed
themselves to get caught up in something like raving; he sees a
culture within a culture getting carried away and then infect-
ing the larger culture with a similar tendency to distort explanations of racial problems. He ponders what has encouraged
black Americans to "conceive of black people as an unofficial
sovereign entity, within which the rules other Americans are
expected to follow are suspended out of a belief that our victimhood renders us morally exempt from them."

Whether we agree with McWhorter or not, he usefully relies on the notion that an entire culture can hurt itself, can lose
control of itself. In the 1990s, several critics of contemporary
feminism had already decried its focus on victimhood, leading
to what they termed "victim feminism." Katie Roiphe, Camille
Paglia, Christina Hoff Sommers, and Naomi Wolf, among others, insisted that women hurt themselves by reinforcing popular images of themselves as preyed upon and cheated. And
shortly before his death in 2003, Columbia University professor and Palestine proponent Edward Said indicated in a letter
published in the *Guardian* that Westerners have been too quick
to accuse Arabs and Muslims of wallowing in victimization.[2]

Sounding a bit like Shelby Steele, McWhorter contends
that by calling themselves victims (instead of victors), African-
Americans make it unlikely they will ever test, let alone

achieve, their full potential. And by ignoring the rules others obey, they only make themselves resented. McWhorter believes that Caucasian-Americans have been cowed into respecting a trumped-up account of black victimhood; he predicts a "white backlash," at which time white Americans will supposedly withdraw much of the moral support they have extended to black Americans, and, further, challenge the entitlement of black Americans to booster benefits such as Affirmative Action. One day the rave will end, he warns, and the bill for it will arrive. In much the same way, the cruelty of Jim Crow laws and lynching of black men ended.

Ultimately, the examples of Caucasian raving resemble those that McWhorter offers and remind us of how forest fires spread. Frenzy can flare up quickly. Beyond that, these various examples challenge us to arbitrate impossibly incoherent contests of victimology in order to determine which minority group has been most oppressed of all.

Another book, *No Crueller Tyrannies,* usefully recounts the misdirected goodwill that swept America in the 1980s and 1990s, as fear of sexual abuse of children clouded the sound judgment of thousands.[3] Dorothy Rabinowitz asks why the public believed the increasingly bizarre accusations of teachers tying naked children to schoolyard trees. Her pieces for the *Wall Street Journal* helped reverse the sentences of five "criminals" accused falsely of sexually molesting children. Rabinowitz argues that parents and bystanders got swooped up in a common passion to see alleged offenders convicted; the horrified sought out one another and came to see themselves as victims as well. Enraged at supposed criminals, they came to live with a new focus and intensity they found intoxicating.

Rabinowitz asks, "How could four-year-olds be raped with butcher knives that left them uninjured?" In terror at having failed to bring their children into a perfect world, one where they could always be protected, parents raved: They created a straw man to attack with relish. Alas, real (and innocent) people had to pay the cost in prison. Parents came to believe that children who insisted nothing had happened to them were simply suppressing the truth. Parents heard only what they wanted to hear. Sympathizing with any person accused of sexually molesting a child violated the progressive views of social liberals and sat uneasily with conservatives. The shadow of a doubt cast by teachers swearing their innocence even provided some nervous parents with a transgressive thrill. At one time, child molestation was a taboo subject in our culture. (Why did that teenage girl's baby look so much like her father? Well, they were white trash, they live like pigs—that's as far as the subject went.) But when it got into the open and anyone could say out loud that children could be raped, and that some had been, parents went hysterical with fear.

Today, a popular passion for equality might be bad for America. Dressing, speaking, and acting like the elite belies the fact that in order for there to be winners, there have to be losers. Grade inflation in high schools and universities reflects the anger of mediocre students who insist that their work is excellent. Misguided sympathy for students who risk self-esteem injuries over non-A grades fails to understand the law of averages. A popular passion for equality unites malcontents of various stripes, who together preach the gospel of a world in which everyone is a diva. Under the rainbow of this utopia, our fears and insecurities feed those of our neighbors. We squeeze out of our minds as best we can the haunting sense that we are doing something that amounts to protesting the laws of gravity.

No Matter What They Say

Sour grapes is an old problem made familiar by the La Fontaine fable of the same name. This phenomenon of reviling what one can't reach partially explains the envious reactions of many hard-working Americans. Ours is still the land of Horatio Alger, of dreams of climbing the ladder of success.

Those of us on lower rungs love to laugh at the higher-ups, the rich and famous, who got to where we didn't. But some of those we scoff at are people whose lives we in fact want deeply for ourselves. That could be us, we think. Raving raises its head here. As Americans, we allow ourselves to think that anything is possible. We can win the lottery if we want to. Our kids can get into Harvard if they try. We can buy a Lexus, a Rolls, a Bentley if we want. We can afford designer clothes and top-of-the-line electronics equipment if we feel like it. Hey, Bill Gates has to use the john, too!

Can we have it all? Can we accomplish anything we set our minds to? More so than ever before in America, we want to think so. Every day, ads on TV and in magazines seem to tell us that we can. We refuse to think about obstacles and the law of probability; we rave. We tell ourselves and others around us that the sky is the limit.

In *The Overspent American,* Juliet Schor blames the seductiveness of advertising, which encourages people to identify with the wealthy then compete with them.[4] In *Luxury Fever,* Robert Frank argues that "The runaway spending at the top has been a virus, one that's spawned a luxury fever that, to one degree or another, has all of us in its grip."[5] Frank writes that recent changes in "the spending environment" have affected the kinds of gifts you must offer at weddings and birthdays, and the amounts you must spend for anniversary dinners; the price you must pay for a house in a neighborhood with a good school; the size your vehicle must be if you want your family to be relatively safe from injury; the kinds of sneakers your children will demand; the universities they'll need to attend if you want them to face good prospects after graduation; the kinds of wine you'll want to serve to mark special occasions; and the kind of suit you'll choose to wear to a job interview.

Competition and stress: These are the building blocks of American culture. The feelings of inadequacy that gnaw at us may have a practical effect: They may urge us in one direction, rather than another. Dissatisfaction with ourselves may prompt us to refashion how we look, how we speak, and how we hope. Best-selling books in recent decades include: *How to Win Friends and Influence People, Seven Habits of Highly Effective People, The Magic of Thinking Big, Think and Grow Rich,* and *How to Have Confidence and Power in Dealing with People.* Costs for an old-fashioned "white wedding" have soared, yet a distressing number of middle- and lower-class couples saddle themselves to considerable debt in order to have one.

In the midst of a growing number of impoverished families in America, the profile of the "pushy parent" becomes more and more familiar. Ambitious parents deserve some praise, certainly, but they rave in an interesting way. They seem determined to prove that their child has enormous potential. "Just because you are my offspring," they seem to say, "you can become a swimming champion and a Princeton graduate." (In fact, many parents are quite modest about their own gifts, but knowledge about DNA and how it works doesn't have much effect on ambitions, hopes, and dreams.) In other cases, reality collides with parents, who then hire experts to document that a child is still brilliant but suffers from a learning disorder. That child then can demand more time to complete tests in school.

This usage of "rave" raises a significant problem. Raving has some deep relationship to transgression. I may be over the line or not, depending on what line is in question, but I am an autonomous being. The pushy parent seems to be neither acting autonomously—there is a kid there—nor obviously transgressing any line. This person is not raving but acting out a fantasy at worst or daydreaming at best.

Here we run up against the limits of a word that itself tests limits. The raving of people who believe they can accomplish the impossible does indeed involve a transgression: self-deception. Lying to ourselves turns out to be just as morally objectionable as lying to others. And yet, lying to ourselves can wildly improve the quality of our lives. For raving may bring real happiness. Deceiving ourselves is a particularly complicated form of raving, but its structure parallels raving's nicely. In raving, we seem to lose control but don't really; in self-deceit, we seem to fool ourselves but don't really.

A little self-deception every now and then is probably a very good thing. Too much of a good thing, though, may lead to absurdity, even an addiction to it. While I want to stretch the notion of raving to include pushy parents or people who generally think themselves capable of anything, it bears noting the difference between addiction and raving. Addiction has not one but two opposites: abstention and raving. In addiction, we simply cannot control ourselves, although we may want to desperately (addictions to drugs, alcohol, food, or sex are more straightforward examples of addiction than pushy parents). In abstention, we succeed in overcoming a desire for something we really want (or used to want). In raving, we can control ourselves but deliberately choose not to. Moreover, we may question the point of controlling ourselves in this particular way.

This is precisely what pushy parents do: They contest the idea that their children possess real limitations. Pushy parents dispute that they are harming their children by inculcating in offspring a lofty sense of possible achievements. Who are they to say whether their kid deserves to get into Harvard?

The stage is set for disappointment and disillusionment in a community in which everyone is above average. We send our children to college in order to bolster, indeed increase, their self-confidence. But what kind of self-confidence is healthy? When does self-confidence become overconfidence? bad faith? We want our children to exhibit poise and confidence, to act as though they are capable of great feats. Capability of achieving greatness, however, means essentially besting others, beating them in competitions. Not everyone can be a winner, the top of the class, the best in the firm.

We set up for disappointment those we love. We no doubt do this to ourselves as well, as in Sophia Loren's advice that nothing makes a woman more beautiful than the belief that she is beautiful. (Though it helps to look like Sophia Loren, for starters.) The blind faith in our talents, our ability to overcome obstacles, is an instance of raving. We want to soar with the high-fliers. But when an actual high-flier (by our own standards) tells us that we are not a high flier, we hold it very much against them.

If raving means losing grip on rationality and moving in a direction that entices us, then self-advancement surely qualifies as a form of raving. This kind of pulling up the anchor from our old identity and casting it forward would seem to be a necessary step toward self-improvement. This means that some raving is a natural part of a healthy life. There is, nonetheless, a ridiculous kind of raving: thinking that anyone, really anyone, has a chance to go to Harvard.

The Best of All Possible Worlds

Americans seem to be going through a national adolescence; they instinctively balk at anything having to do with an always suspect ruling class, while at the same time yearning to overtake that ruling class.

The problem I'm describing is akin to a college seminar in which all students hope to finish with an "A" grade. Some of those students who do not earn the highest mark in the class will complain to the teacher, protesting unfairness of some sort, or a simple error of judgment. The spirit of such criticism parallels various attacks on standardized tests such as the SAT and LSAT as intrinsically biased (in favor of a particular class and/or race).

Thomas Sowell analyzes the contemporary American will to power in *The Quest for Cosmic Justice*. Sowell points out that defining equality (or establishing superiority and inferiority) is ultimately a conceptual dilemma: Statistics cannot capture the complexity of multidimensional variables used to measure how well off we are, relative to one another (for example, a person making next to no money for three consecutive years may be a well-educated entrepreneur on the brink of making his or her fortune). Vast disparities in performances of individuals persist; these disparities stem from different variables, including economic, racial, and technological. American success at lifting recurrent waves of destitute immigrants into the middle class in the nineteenth and twentieth centuries fueled unbounded optimism, the price of which is only now registering on the social compass.

As Sowell has observed, "The most sweeping denials of performance superiority have been based on redefining them out of existence as culturally biased 'perceptions' and 'stereotypes.' Those who take this approach of cultural relativism acknowledge only differences but no superiority."[6] But Sowell asserts that studying the history of discrete cultures and individuals will inevitably destroy the conviction that we are all similarly endowed with potential for excellence of any kind.

I agree with Sowell that performance equality is the most difficult of all kinds of equality to believe in. He considers wholly unsubstantiated the prevailing assumption in America that the world would be random or even, in the absence of discrimination or bias by individuals, institutions, or "society." He maintains that, "the desired state of equality itself is not the real issue, especially since such a state of equality seems very unlikely to be achieved. What is crucial are the processes set in motion in hopes of approaching that state."

Sounding much like John McWhorter, Sowell stresses that cultures have consequences. Ignoring those consequences while proclaiming equality as a self-justifying ideal does nothing to benefit the less fortunate and, in fact, tends to freeze them into their backward position while the rest of the world advances. The bitter irony is that all this philosophical self-indulgence widens the empirical gap in the name of narrowing it. As corroboration, Sowell offers the observation that Latinos who speak English earn higher incomes than Latinos who speak only Spanish. As an even more compelling example, he asks us to consider Japan, which painfully realized its backwardness in the nineteenth century. Instead of denying its problem or defining it away, Japan worked hard to move forward and transformed itself into a technological powerhouse in the late twentieth century.

Sowell argues compellingly for the sad but inevitable conclusion that talent of any sort is distributed unequally among people. No conceivable redistribution of wealth or prestige will satisfy everyone. Most Americans learn this lesson at least by the end of high school. Although we may yearn for a utopian society in which no one is any more talented than anyone else, we know such a world does not exist. Frankly, the world we have, while sadder in some important respect, is probably quite a bit more interesting.

We Americans rave when we band together and protest standardized examinations that judge some students intellectually superior to others. We rave when we scour the hiring history of a firm or company and insist on finding a bias we object to strenuously. Maybe the bias is there, maybe not. But by fooling ourselves together, by savoring the power splinter groups can wield over established institutions, we rave. We lose sight of what we learned back in high school: There will always be losers in every social world we visit, and sometimes the losers will look just like us. This is not to say that a loser today is a loser forever, only to suggest that the loser may have him- or herself to blame more that we may be prepared to admit while caught up in collective sympathy.

By no means is the delicate state of a reach exceeding its grasp limited to one demographic group. At one time or another, each of us hopes that others will take us at our own extravagant self-valuation. When we band together and try to have our way, we take a chance on fooling all the people all the time.

Self-esteem v. Omnipotence

Raving illustrates the irrational underside of self-esteem. Many of us pretend to be something we're not; we lose sight of reality and revel in the feeling. Along with the positive aspects of transgressing, raving has a downside as well.

Self-esteem ebbs and rises throughout our lives. Unstable, it can desert us suddenly. Its stay is usually temporary, although not so temporary as raving. Nonetheless, we expect self-esteem to return to us when we lack it, just as we expect to return to control when we rave. Because we miss self-esteem painfully, we may artificially hoist up our self-estimation. In doing so, we hope that others will be persuaded to think more highly of us.

In virtually every American high school, a significant number of kids will play the roles of beauty queen, athletic hero, genius, etc. But not just there: in the office, in the health club, on the PTA. This ranking takes place in a world in which almost everything about us can be measured and quantified on the Internet, in the science or psychology lab, or on television. A world of endless athletic competitions, political contests, awards ceremonies, and the like ought to bring each person to understand that only one person or one team can be number one.

And yet so many people pretend that they are number one! Moderately talented athletes strut and talk as though they have a chance at playing in the NFL. Somewhat attractive men and women hold themselves as though they could be New York models. We might call this the "everything is beautiful" phenomenon, which runs through a world in which every person is not only above average, but downright exceptional. "If you're so smart, why didn't you go to Princeton?" we might ask. The last thing "wannabe" snobs can tolerate is being outdone. They will call us snobs or retort that we are simply cruel if we try to probe their reasons for believing what they seem to about themselves (and what they want us to believe about them).

In a viciously competitive culture such as America's, children are conditioned to equate self-esteem with omnipotence. They learn to rave. Raving can be quite confusing, for it amounts to informed irrationality. Raving plays a crucial role, not just in individual accomplishment but in a competitive culture. Unless we let go of the fear of failure, cut loose the trappings of reality, we cannot aspire to what is currently beyond our apparent grasp. We must pretend we are someone else in order to become the person we want to be. This is, after all, the American way.

Mere Mortals

In his memoirs, the Romanian-French playwright Eugene Ionesco wrote, "The only thing I have left is my regret at being someone else. It is this regret that makes me continue to be myself...."[7] His regret over aging indicates a wish to inhabit the body of his younger self. A deeper regret at not being someone else surfaces in Nietzsche's *On the Genealogy of Morals*:

> Where does one not encounter that veiled glance which burdens one with a profound sadness, that inward-turned glance of the born failure which betrays how such people speak to themselves—that glance which is a sigh! "If only I were someone else," sighs that glance: "but there is no hope of that. I am who I am: how could I ever get free of myself? And yet—I am sick of myself!" (*GM* III, Section 14)

Several decades earlier before Nietzsche, Schopenhauer had written of the "bitterest of all human sufferings, dissatisfaction with our own individuality."[8] Wanting to *be* someone else signals something terribly wrong. It is one thing to want to *have* something someone else possesses (for example, a car, a house, membership in a particular club), but it is quite another thing to want to step outside of ourselves.

I have been arguing throughout this book that there is nothing wrong with the desire to transcend ourselves for a while, to forget for a moment or a night what it is we feel belittles or traps us. I have been talking about reaching a place often referred to as ecstasy. This destination differs from trying to assume the identity of someone we envy. On some level, envy and its effects resemble raving, to the extent that both lead us away from a focus on ourselves. Raving provides a way of "trying on" a new identity: This experience of being another person is part of raving.

Earlier I mentioned Kant's imperative that we shun the life of a couch potato and develop our talents. The problem with such a view is that it presupposes that we all have talents. A great many of us have limited talents indeed. And so how do rise to meet the imperative of Kant? If leading a moral life requires us to become all that we can be, then failure assumes a crucial role in our development. Through failure, we would seem to satisfy Kant's requirement. Failure proves that we've gone as far as we can go in a world in which there can only be a few winners.

But is this so? The problem with granting failure such power comes from the old maxim, "If at first you don't succeed, then try, try again" and the typically American refusal to take "no" for an answer. The corporate world does not tolerate failure; it ruthlessly fires executives and managers who do not meet goals. The same is true in the world of professional sports, where coaches and star players labor under the anxiety of losing their jobs all the time. Hubris, condemned in the ancient Greek world, commands real respect in America these days.

Again, the answer may well be that a certain amount of self-deceit is necessary to survive in an increasingly competitive world. Surely not everyone can get into Princeton, but you have to work as though you will be one of the chosen few in order to amass a record that even makes you look like a candidate for Princeton. This kind of irrationality or self-deceit plays into raving. When all the world tells you how unlikely it is that you will ever play Wimbledon, you must abandon common sense and spread your wings. Gritting your teeth, you lose control in what will earn you great praise if you attain your goal and elicit sneers from others if you fail. As the song from *South Pacific* goes, "If you don't have a dream, how you gonna have a dream come true?"

The things we can't do fall roughly into two categories: those due to internal limitations (insufficient intelligence or perseverance, for example) and those due to external limitations (discrimination against women and racial minorities, for example). True, social institutions and prejudice sometimes stand in the way and block very talented people from getting what they want. And damaged self-respect may be a function of oppression. But sometimes people are themselves the reason for failure. The old Italian saying *"volere e potere"* ("to will something is to be able to do it") breaks down in test runs. We would do well to remember that there are many schools out there besides Harvard and Princeton, many contests in life besides Oscars, Grammys, Tonys, and Olympic gold. There are worlds of things to have or lose, to get into or not get into. It's up to each of us to keep our sense of perspective.

Raving Together

And yet measured raving, for all its moral ambiguity, can insulate us against full-scale self-destruction. Part of the reason American capitalism continues to work so well is that it allows everyone to hope for a windfall. Provided that we keep an eye on the ground beneath us, raving has much to teach us. Through raving, we learn why limitations on our desires pass from one generation to another. And through raving, we discover a powerful bond to people around us. Throughout most of this book, I have presented raving as a private affair, a function of what we do to or with ourselves. But we should see quickly that others may be "harming" themselves in the same way we are, and at the same time.

Group raving occurs on both a conscious and unconscious level, as do efforts to resolve it. Mass raving is not exactly fun, but it is certainly pleasurable. We enjoy a fresh and intense bond with our neighbors. Mass raving can explain why Americans now seem so keen to paint all its citizens as a star. Graduation ceremonies for kindergartners and protests against the SAT belie a throbbing pain deep within American culture. Alas, the most powerful country in the world sifts out the strong from the very strong and distributes rewards accordingly. Those left wanting feel understandably awful. So begins the passionate campaign for equality, which used to pertain to opportunities, but which now increasingly pertains to performance. A relatively lackluster performance means someone must have suffered a lack of opportunities.

Americans hunger for opportunities to rave together. Much like the frenzy that overtakes spectators at football matches, collective raving fills us with rapture, lifts us out of ourselves, momentarily erases all awareness of our inadequacies. Charismatic religious services, sexual passion, and recreational drug use approximate this collective ecstasy, when we escape ourselves with glee. But the moment cannot last. That all ecstasy passes, however, does not discount the worth of it. The burning question remains, rather, the cost of it. We harm life's winners by insisting that they allow losers to stand beside them on the medals platform. We harm ourselves by restraining the winners in our midst who could lead the rest of us to dizzying new heights.

Absent without Leave

WHAT'S BAD FOR US POINTS THE WAY TO WHAT'S GOOD for us. When we disagree with the world around us, we will often go absent without leave. This is what raving amounts to. Raving brings out into the open what people think of us. Raving is the linguistic equivalent of red lights that flash at us: "You are entering a danger zone. You may proceed if you wish, but only because we cannot legally stop you. Turn around now." Raving is all to the good, but you'll have no one but yourself to blame for any thorny consequences.

Refusing to obey the directives of our communities can unleash terrible consequences, such as humiliation and bankruptcy. Refusing to respect the limits of our bodies can cost us our lives; Jimi Hendrix and Janis Joplin are only two of thousands of drug users who simply went too far. How many people have died from jumping out of planes on skydiving adventures? Or from bungee jumping? How many people have suffered humiliation from failed plastic surgery or Botox injections? Masochists aside, self-harm is rarely the goal of raving. Pleasure is what's at issue, and personal security is the risk we accept in the name of liberation, gratification, or growth.

The two adages on which we should focus as we ponder our capacity to do ourselves in are: 1) Vanity, vanity, all is vanity! and 2) Curiosity killed the cat. Social limits erected between what we may or may not do to ourselves hold great explanatory power. In our encounter with them, we create ourselves. Leapfrogging over restraints may produce the joy of self-discovery; deliberately staying away from them may produce the joy of self-mastery. Charles Taylor has argued that "stepping outside these limits would be tantamount to stepping outside what we would recognize as integral, that is, undamaged human personhood."[1] I have argued that some rules are made to be broken, not in order to *do* something specific but rather to *feel* something life-giving.

The theory overreaches when it tries to explain a vast number of examples across cultures and centuries. Certain trespasses pertain to the here and now, that is, North America and Western Europe in the new century: having unprotected sex with partners at high risk for AIDS or provoking police officers into killing you (sometimes called "suicide by cop," this is a curious phenomenon that accounts for nearly 10 percent of fatal police shootings in the United States). Or take a desperate attempt to regain self-control after sexual abuse, a case that demands sensitivity of judgment. A man or a woman abused as a child may crave a sense of body control and then begin to act out sexually. The compulsiveness of the promiscuous may disguise a genuine effort to demonstrate self-control, albeit in a twisted fashion. Other examples bridge time and place: handling poisonous snakes and provoking rage in people known to be physically violent (the so-called victim-precipitated homicide). This book covered stranger examples of self-harm (for example, masturbatory adventures that turn fatal and the yearning to be an amputee), the very bizarreness of which somehow made the lure of self-exploration more urgent. The siren song of the traitor within unleashes a delicious rush of beta-endorphins, we scientists may conclude today. An old-fashioned thrill finds itself described in biological terms that still fail to establish precisely why we accept the risk of self-harm.

A modern culture that glorifies the self hides from ready view the distaste in which many of us occasionally hold ourselves. We may ache to bust out of a self that does not entirely satisfy us, particularly in an age when the self basks in a light that used to shine exclusively on God. Self-destructive behavior may be a means of manipulating others, or it may simply indicate an effort to strengthen or ramp up a depleted self. Freud reduced self-hurt to a biology of drives and psycho-pathology, but the key to understanding self-harm may be as simple as needing a vacation.

Hard-working people, be they peasants in the field or Wall Street powerbrokers, don't tend to take vacations. Peasants don't have many vacation options, but they have to stifle their adventurous urges almost as regularly as the corporate titans do. And so the hungry self becomes a distracting, poten-tially disrupting force. Muslim ascetics have thought of *jihad* first and foremost as combat against an internal threat: the self, oozing with appetites and fantasies. Even the most self-disciplined, however, eventually overflow their confines, if only momentarily. Raving, hardly a case of masochism, mir-rors a cup that overfloweth. A celebration that may be brief, short-lived, or silly, raving is a celebration nonetheless. We can't take the vacations we may want to take; we can't stave off old age, death, and disillusion; but we can rave.

In medieval demonology, the devil robs people of their self-control. Today, the desire for fame does. Humiliation has prompted the recent genre of reality TV shows. Of course, that kind of humiliation happens to someone else, not us. We ar-guably debase ourselves, though, just by watching reality TV, or staring wide-eyed at MTV all day and allowing ourselves to fall under its spell, much as people get lost in surfing the Internet.

Naughtiness is self-indulgence; its rebelliousness does not aim for righting social injustices (such as abolitionists working on the underground railroad during the American Civil War, or Socrates holding his ground against angry Athenians). Self-indulgence often offends others. But because all self-creation turns on self-indulgence, we can't condemn raving out of hand. Our neighbors value independence as much as we do. Raving grows protected in the shadow of independence.

One cannot be a self on one's own. We need others. Rules

bind us to others. When we break rules, we strain our ties to others. If there were no rules to break, we couldn't rave, we could only enjoy ourselves ordinarily. Falling in love doesn't involve breaking a rule, yet the feeling of being swept away in romance can yield a feeling similar to the one that emerges from deliberately, affirmatively breaking a rule. Naughtiness hovers over rules we consider suspendable, particularly those rules governing our relations to ourselves.

The personal freedom that others choose to allow us peters out at the threshold of raving. Raving answers the questions of what we can get away with morally and, consequently, how free we can be. By defining raving simply as a form of resistance, we'd run the risk finding it everywhere. I have tried to fill out a narrower form of defiance that turns on self-discovery and self-fulfillment. If we think of raving not as a means of resisting authority but rather as a way of exercising it, then it will be easier to understand some of the contested decisions we make. Moral transgression seems not just more human but more rational when we allow that a person might reasonably decline uninterrupted self-control. Raving makes us think again about the morality of self-control: Does morality necessarily require the self-control? Yes, but only if we acknowledge two separate dimensions of self-control: self-regulation (when I say no to myself) and self-dominion (when others withhold the right for me to say yes to myself). It's this second meaning that makes raving so tricky: We feel we belong to ourselves and therefore are entitled to do as we please with both body and future.

Raving stands between sanity and madness as purgatory stands between heaven and hell. Part of what frightens others about our raving is uncertainty over whether we can or will stop ourselves.

What are we thinking when we rave? We bask in danger and say to ourselves: "Take the plunge, hope for the best." We wish never to be found out, never to pay the consequences. This orchestrated self-deception is not altogether ridiculous because, statistically, we have a fair shot of success. The majority of misdeeds are never brought to light. Plenty of scandals wait to be discovered, and it is this fact that keeps gossip columnists in business.

Raving raises the question of whether we are dangerous just to ourselves or to others as well. Our individual raving may ripple through our neighborhoods and create bands of fellow travelers. We have regularly heard the death knell sound for the end of science, the end of philosophy, the end of morality, the end of literature, the end of theology, even for the end of culture. Raving sets off these alarms.

What is raving? It is the judgment we pass on actions and ideas likely to confuse or contradict reigning views of how the world should work, how individuals should behave. It overlaps with the realm of what is illegal, what can land you in prison. But it often stands apart from the illegal and signals what we wish *were* illegal. Essentially, raving represents ways in which we bend the rules, as opposed to break them. However, since it does involve what others define as outright transgression, some will consider raving itself a moral trespass.

Raving as both an idea and an action falls under the category of morality: Raving amounts to a moral challenge to virtue. Virtue does not just happen. It begins with self-control. We worry that others who cannot control themselves cannot manage to lead a moral life. So much madness in the world, and so many ways to fall apart. We prove to the world that we are holding up our part of the social contract by demonstrating control in the face of chaos.

The paradox of raving is that we govern our loss of control. Although it appears to others that we have lost control, we haven't. It's a temporary state, much as the free-fall of a roller coaster or a plunging ride at the amusement park. Were we to lose total control, as in addiction or manic depression, we would not enjoy the ride. Ravers differ from all-the-way-to-the-enders by virtue of an ability to stop, to pull back from the brink of disaster. To exercise self-control.

Stories we heard as children condition us to associate flying with control and falling with trouble. Falling into ourselves after flights into morality and repressive social codes can thrill us. Even strong birds soaring in the sky will often choose to fall toward the earth, only to break their descent before hitting ground. We do the same in raving.

Although raving can be quite solitary, the very idea of raving only makes sense within a social order. When existential philosophy, with its emphasis on the absurd, became popular among artists and intellectuals in the mid-twentieth century, in the ashes of World War II, there didn't seem to remain a context in which to discuss raving. In a world pervaded with malaise, uncertainty, and displacement, everything looked like raving.

In the twenty-first century, existentialism no longer commands much of a following. Technology imposes a world order on the globe, and technology has no time for philosophical formulations of the ridiculousness of human interaction. There is work to be done. Precisely because there is so much work to be done, though, we dream of breaking free. The urge to let off steam stretches back for millennia. The urge to enjoy ourselves, instead of getting work done or demonstrating our capacity for moral behavior, shares something important with the ambition to make something of our lives. Self-fulfillment lies at the end of both enjoyment and disciplined devotion to a goal.

Self-fulfillment isn't always good. We applaud the idea of a hero working to realize his or her goals, but we hate the idea of a villain doing the same. This leads us to the problem of raving: The exhilaration it promises relies on transgression. How do we fit terrorism into our lives, for instance? Specifically, how do we make sense of those young people who find self-fulfillment in terrorist training camps, often to their parents' surprise and dismay? At what point in their lives did raving become ravaging? At what point could they perhaps have been brought back and made to see that the transgressive has become evil? This is something we global technocrats must seriously consider in our new century. This book reaches climax in the puzzling mindset of the terrorist, the suicide bomber.

Raving can also describe letting go, a mental move. Before giving in to temptation, we struggle. Sin, transgression beckon us. We hesitate, then we fall. We land just where we want to be, although we may later regret the fall. If we subsequently excuse the act as raving, we join others in condemnation of ourselves. We forget or fail to realize the good of raving, the point of challenging our tradition before internalizing it. Regret will accompany raving only if we change our minds about what we've done. Raving underlies the insanity defense used in modern courtrooms; it also comes in handy when we try to explain to others why we keep making the exact same mistake in our personal lives. We defend ourselves at a certain cost: making raving sound like a weakness. We lose a part of ourselves when we disown our inclinations.

The world has punished raving. This is understandable. Raving represents a retreat into the self, which has been taken as a mark of selfishness. Adults who consciously choose not to have children are accused of selfishness, for example. Solitary pursuits—indeed the earnest attempt to find oneself—can get us into trouble socially. On some level, our neighbors really do disapprove of solitude. This disapproval will manifest itself in the most interesting and dramatic ways in the twenty-first century: Our communities will be able to track down every thought we have ever expressed on the Internet, and to ascertain our genetic makeup, in the likelihood that we will die in a particular way or suffer from particular ailments. Now as ever, it is dangerous for us to show too much enthusiasm for solitude.

Because fighting against the rest of the world seems to do so little good, there is a strong incentive for giving in to the expectations of others. So much of the world seems to be beyond our control that we want to prove that we can at least control ourselves. Unfortunately, doing so seems less and less possible.

A century ago, Freud told us that unconscious urges dictate the course of our lives. Half a century before that, Marx wrote that the dialectic of history determined our paths, while Darwin argued it was natural selection. More recently, research has emerged to show how chemicals in our brains will govern our happiness. As we mature, it may seem less and less likely that we will conquer the world and more likely that it will conquer us. In response, we may insist on the importance of raving, of pushing the world back away from us.

I have tried to present raving as a strength, a mark of an individual consciously liberating him- or herself from a restrictive culture. Our culture has evolved dramatically since Romantic thinkers set themselves to restoring our sense of awe some two centuries ago. Sometimes it seems that industrial and technological advances have tamed too much of the world, that there's no mystery anymore. Raving, we think, may lead us to the mystery that could still exist somewhere. Sex and religious experiences deliver glimpses of such a mysterious paradise. Both pull us out of ourselves, which is the start of trouble.

To say that we lose ourselves when we lose self-control is to raise a difficult question about personality. Who are we? Is our self-control our identity? Raving is a decision we make. Part of the paradox of enjoying the loss of control is that we don't really lose control. We just let go of it for a little while. If we couldn't regain control, if we became a slave to an addiction, we wouldn't find any pleasure in the raving slide. Gambling responsibly, for example, may thrill us. Gambling more and more often, though, and losing money regularly, may start to trouble us. We may try to deny we have a problem.

We deceive ourselves by playing at how the world looks to us. Self-deception, though not always ethically reprehensible, always makes us feel better (at least a little) than we otherwise would. It can get us into a lot of trouble, though. We may, for example, tell ourselves that we are capable of virtually any achievement. Later, we may angrily hold the world responsible for our own misjudgment.

Ultimately, the reason we will decide to forego raving comes down to self-interest. Freedom, Janis Joplin reminds us in the popular song "Me and Bobby McGee," is sometimes what we find when we have nothing left to lose. When we value things and have much to lose, we must limit our freedom. We cannot allow ourselves to rave.

Back and forth, back and forth: Raving yields both positive and negative consequences. If we are ever going to achieve anything notable, we will have to break out of the ordinary, the day-to-day thinking that characterizes so much of human interaction. We will have to tell ourselves a far-fetched story in order to catapult from the ghetto to the Broadway stage. Raving can work wonders in our lives.

When we rave, though, we take leave of others. Usually we do this without their approval or, even, permission. Raving is perhaps best understood in terms of the military alert "absent without leave." We haven't been taken captive, we've willingly left the ranks to find ourselves beyond the troops. When we return, we'll have some explaining to do. The scolding we'll get will only be for our own good, after all.

acknowledgments

GAYATRI PATNAIK PROVIDED EXPERT ASSISTANCE AS WELL as constant enthusiasm for this project. She makes the job of editor look easy. Christopher Vyce, an assistant editor at Beacon, contributed much to this book, as did Helene Atwan, the director of the Press. Diane Gibbons, who also edited the manuscript, exceeded all expectations—just as I had expected. I am pleased to have collaborated with fine editors, particularly Gayatri.

Jack Schlegel read an early draft of the book and showered me with suggestions and encouragement, as did Aaron Ben Ze-ev. David Lenson read the manuscript for Beacon Press and delivered a thoroughly intelligent reader's report. Jerome Neu read the chapter "The Men of UVa" and offered useful comments.

notes

Preface: Where the Wild Things Are

1. See Wendy Nothcutt, *The Darwin Awards: Evolution in Action* (New York: Plume, 2002).

2. Deborah Shapley, *Promise and Power: The Life and Times of Robert McNamara* (Boston: Little, Brown, 1993), 354.

3. Neil MacFarquhar, "Human Shields, No Resume Needed," *New York Times*, 21 February 2003, A1. I borrow extensively from MacFarquhar in this paragraph.

Chapter One: Bad for Us

1. In 1937, the National Socialists mounted an exhibition in Munich called *Entartete Kunst* (Degenerate Art), which assembled more than 650 paintings, sculptures, prints, and books. See Stephanie Barron, *Degenerate Art: The Fate of the Avant-garde in Nazi Germany* (New York: Abrams, 1991).

2. Leon E. Wynter, *American Skin: Pop Culture, Big Business, and the End of White America* (New York: Crown, 2002).

3. Bernard Weinraub, "As Taboo Fades, Actors See Little Career Jeopardy in Playing Gay Characters," *New York Times*, 11 September 1997, C11. In June 2003, the American television star Richard Chamberlain publicly revealed that he is gay. At the age of sixty-five, and with few movie offers, he said he finally felt safe to embrace his sexuality. Americans yawned at the revelation; it was hard to shock them with homosexuality by that time.

4. Richard Schmiechen, *Changing Our Minds: The Story of Dr. Evelyn Hooker* (San Francisco: Frameline, 1992).

5. Amy Harmon, "On-line Dating Sheds Its Stigma as Losers.com," *New York Times*, 28 June 2003.

Chapter Two: Are We Not Our Own?

1. Augustine, *Confessions,* trans. R. S. Pine-Coffin (New York: Penguin, 1961), 223.

2. Gore Vidal, *Hollywood* (New York: Vintage, 1990), 208.

3. James Carroll, from *An American Requiem* (Boston: Houghton Mifflin, 1996). Quoted in Marilyn Sewell, ed., *Resurrecting Grace: Remembering Catholic Childhoods* (Boston: Beacon Press, 2001), 183.

4. Norbert Elias, *The Civilizing Process: The Development of Manners* (New York: Urizen Books, 1978), Michel Foucault sketches the emergence of an ancient Greek focus on the self in *The Care of the Self,* trans. Robert Hurley (New York: Vintage, 1986).

5. Frank Browning, *The Culture of Desire* (New York: Vintage, 1994), 116.

6. Ian F. Haney López, "Institutional Racism: Judicial Conduct and a New Theory of Racial Discrimination," in *Yale Law Journal,* vol. 109, no. 8 (June 2000), 1800–1.

7. This list comes from Kant's *Metaphysics of Morals* (6:423–6:462). See Alan Wood, *Kant's Ethical Thought* (New York: Cambridge University Press, 1999), 140–41.

8. Immanuel Kant, *Groundwork of the Metaphysics of Morals,* trans. H. J. Paton (New York: Harper & Row, 1964), 96–7.

9. Immanuel Kant, *Lectures on Ethics,* 118–19. Kant, who never married, supposedly enjoyed dressing up in frilly clothes and gossiping with the ladies around town. See Manfred Kuehn, *Kant: A Biography* (New York: Cambridge University Press, 2001).

10. Kant, *Lectures on Ethics,* 122–23.

11. Robert P. George, "Individual Rights, Collective Interests, Public Law, and American Politics," in *Natural Law,* John Finnis, ed. (Aldershot: Dartmouth, 1991), vol. 2, 105.

12. See David Boaz, *Libertarianism: A Primer* (New York: Free Press, 1997), 246–48. This summary comes largely from Boaz.

Chapter Three: Flights of Fancy

1. See P. Taylor, " 'My Left Foot Was Not Part of Me,' " *The Guardian,* 6 February 2000, 14; Clare Dyer, "Surgeon Amputated Healthy Legs," *British Medical Journal,* 320 (5 February 2000), 332; Stephen McGinty and Sue Leonard,

"Secret World of Would-Be Amputees," *Sunday Times*, 6 February 2000. See especially Carl Elliott's analysis in *Better Than Well: American Medicine Meets the American Dream* (New York: W. W. Norton, 2003), chapter 9.

2. See Mark Landler, "German Man Arrested in a Case of Homicide and Cannibalism," *New York Times*, 18 December 2002, A15; Alan Hall, "German Net Cannibal had Londoner on Menu," *Times* (London), 24 July 2003; and " 'I Longed for a Brother,' Says Cannibal at Trial," *Times* (London), 3 December 2003.

3. For a hilarious account of how priests in the Middle Ages used to trap young boys into confessing the grave sin of masturbation, see Thomas N. Tentler, *Sin and Confession on the Eve of the Reformation* (Princeton: Princeton University Press, 1977), 91–92.

4. For an extended account of how a vast array of people have argued that dancing harms us, see Ann Wagner, *Adversaries of Dance: From the Puritans to the Present* (Urbana: University of Illinois Press, 1997).

5. There are a number of gripping histories of masturbation, its disastrous social consequences, and even of historical records of families turning over one of their own to authorities. See Ann Goldberg's chapter "Masturbatory Insanity and Delinquency" in *Sex, Religion, and the Making of Modern Madness* (New York: Oxford University Press, 1999); Peter Allen Lewis, *The Wages of Sin: Sex and Disease, Past and Present* (Chicago: University of Chicago Press, 2000), chapter 5; and Thomas Laqueur, *Solitary Sex: A Cultural History of Masturbation* (New York: Zone Books, 2003).

6. Quoted in Uta Ranke-Heinemann, *Eunuchs for the Kingdom of Heaven: Women, Sexuality, and the Catholic Church*, trans. Peter Heinegg (New York: Penguin, 1990), 317.

7. John Donald Gustav-Wrathall, *Take the Young Stranger by the Hand: Same-Sex Relations and the YMCA* (Chicago: University of Chicago Press, 1998), 176–77.

8. James A. Brundage, *Law, Sex, and Society in Medieval Europe* (Chicago: University of Chicago Press, 1987), 534. Philosophers and theologians have largely neglected female masturbation. For a lively history of the vibrator, see Rachel P. Maines, *The Technology of Orgasm* (Baltimore: Johns Hopkins University Press, 1999), especially 56–59.

9. Bernard Häring, *The Law of Christ*, trans. Edwin G. Kaiser (Westminster, M.D.: The Newman Press, 1966), vol. 3, 301–2.

10. Robert Burton, *The Anatomy of Melancholy*, Floyd Dell and Paul Jordan Smith, eds. (New York: Farrar and Rinehart, 1927), 355.

11. See Robert R. Hazelwood, Park Elliott Dietz, Ann Wolbert Burgess, *Auto-Erotic Fatalities* (Lexington, Mass.: Lexington Books, 1983). Dietz contends that physicians and historians routinely misrepresented or misclassified boys who died like this; these boys were not "experimenting with ropes," nor had they been "reenacting some cowboy film on television."

12. Denise Danks, *The Pizza House Crash* (London: Orion, 1989).

13. In *Critchlow v. First UNUM Life Insurance Company of America,* No. 00-CV-6168L (W.D.N.Y. 29 March 2002), Chief Judge David G. Larimer found that the decedent's death fell within a policy's exclusion for intentionally self-inflicted injuries and granted the defendant insurance company's motion for summary judgment dismissing the complaint. UNUM contended that plaintiff was not entitled to benefits because of the exclusion for "intentionally self-inflicted injuries." See also *Cronin v. Zurich American Insurance.* On October 8, 1998, on a business trip for his employer A. T. Kearney, Inc., Phillip Cronin was discovered dead in his hotel room in Helsinki, Finland. Cronin was found hanging by his neck, suspended from a luggage strap looped to a hook on the bathroom door. Immediately prior to his death, Mr. Cronin had been masturbating. The insurance company refused to provide Cronin's widow with death benefits; she sued the insurance company and lost.

14. "Can masturbating each day keep the doctor away?," *New Scientist,* 19 July 2003, 15.

15. Betty Dodson, *Sex for One: The Joy of Selfloving* (New York: Random House, 1995).

16. Gustav-Wrathall, *Take the Young Stranger by the Hand* (Chicago: University of Chicago Press, 1998), 23.

17. Mary Douglas, *Natural Symbols: Explorations in Cosmology,* rev. ed. (London: Barrie and Jenkins, 1973), 12.

18. See the interview recorded at http://www.abc.net.au/worldtoday/s39998.htm.

19. G. W. F. Hegel, *Philosophy of Right* (1821), T. M. Knox, trans. (Oxford: Clarendon Press, 1952), 53.

20. Paul Theroux, "Nurse Wolf," *The New Yorker,* 15 June 1998, 50–60.

21. John Stuart Mill, *On Liberty,* David Spitz, ed. (New York: W. W. Norton, 1975), 95.

22. John D. Hodson, "Mill, Paternalism, and Slavery" in *Analysis* 41 (January

1981), 60–62. See also Joel Feinberg, "Legal Paternalism" in *Canadian Journal of Philosophy* I (1971), 118–20; Tom L. Beauchamp, "Paternalism and Biobehavioral Control," in *The Monist* 60 (1977), 74; and Michael Bayles, *Principles of Legislation* (Detroit: Wayne State University Press, 1978), 130. For a concise discussion of moral objections to selling oneself into slavery, see Joel Feinberg, *Harm to Self* (New York: Oxford University Press, 1984), 79–81.

23. Stephanie Strom, "Organ Donor's Generosity Raises Question of How Much Is Too Much," *New York Times,* 17 August 2003, A14. For a similar study of extraordinary selflessness, see Philip J. Hilts, "French Doctor Testing AIDS Vaccine on Self," *Washington Post,* 19 March 1987, A1. For an engaging study of self-experimentation, see Lawrence K. Altman, *Who Goes First: The Story of Self-Experimentation in Medicine* (New York: Random House, 1987).

24. Helen Rumblow, "Fallen Men: At 'John School,' Students Review a Lesson Picked Up on the Street," *Washington Post,* 28 August 2002, C1, C4.

25. See Linton Weeks, "Web Site for Voyeur Eyes: Jenni Has a Camera in Her Room," *Washington Post,* 20 September 1997, H1.

26. Not everyone appreciated the Jennicam. Tele-Communications Inc. president Leo Hindery, Jr., cited Jennicam as "an example of the moral dangers of the Internet." See Timothy Hanrahan, "Slice of Life on Web's Jennicam Is Deemed Too Raw by One Critic," *Wall Street Journal,* 31 March 1998, B1.

27. Elisabeth Eaves, *Bare: On Women, Dancing, Sex, and Power* (New York: Knopf, 2002), 284.

28. See Sheila Jeffreys, *The Idea of Prostitution* (Australia: Spinifex, 1998). Jeffreys opposes prostitution but includes narratives of prostitutes who praise their profession. A collection of sex worker perspectives can be found in Frederique Delacoste and Priscilla Alexander, eds., *Sex Work: Writings by Women in the Sex Industry* (San Francisco: Cleis Press, 1987). The Internet is a good source of narratives by men who claim to enjoy buying sex. The Swiss sculptor Alberto Giacometti could apparently enjoy sex only if his (female) partner were a prostitute.

29. See David Richards, "Commercial Sex and the Rights of the Person: A Moral Argument for the Decriminalization of Prostitution," *University of Pennsylvania Law Review* 127 (1995), 1195, 1269–70; Lars Ericsson, "Charges Against Prostitution," *Ethics* 90 (1980), 335–66; and Linda R. Hirshman and Jane E. Larson, *Hard Bargains: The Politics of Sex* (New York: Oxford University Press, 1998). This last summary has been particularly helpful, and I follow it closely here.

30. Andrew Sean Greer, *How It Was for Me* (New York: Picador, 2000).

31. Peter Gay, *The Tender Passion: The Bourgeois Experience, Victoria to Freud* (New York: W. W. Norton, 1999), 265.

32. Joshua Gamson, *Freaks Talk Back: Tabloid Talk Shows and Sexual Nonconformity* (Chicago: University of Chicago Press, 1998), 6. Here I borrow from his introduction, "Why I Love Trash." His insights are deepened in a subsequent work by the same press; see Laura Grindstaff, *The Money Shot: Trash, Class, and the Making of TV Talk Shows* (Chicago: University of Chicago Press, 2002).

33. Writing in 1998, Gamson chronicled some of the topics of the last few years: "lipstick lesbians," gay teens, lesbian cops, cross-dressing hookers, transsexual call girls, gay and lesbian gang members, straight go-go dancers pretending to be gay, people who want their relatives to stop cross-dressing, lesbian and gay comedians, gay people in love with straight people, women who love gay men, lesbian mothers, gay beauty pageants, transsexual beauty pageants, people who are fired for not being gay, gay men reuniting with their high school sweethearts, bisexual couples, gays in the military, same-sex crushes, boys who want to be girls, male-to-female transsexuals and their boyfriends, and gay talk shows. What a list! If anything will make homosexuality seem trite, talk shows will.

34. Quoted in Janice Kaplan, "Are Talk Shows out of Control?" *TV Guide*, 1 April 1995, 12.

35. See Jeffrey Gettleman, "In North Carolina, the 2-Tiara State, a Beauty of a Fight," *New York Times*, 6 September 2002, A1.

36. See Lynn Hirschberg, "Sitcom, Murder, Pornographic Web Site. Now, the Hollywood Biopic!," *New York Times*, 29 September 2002.

37. Harold Bloom, *How to Read and Why* (New York: Scribner, 2000).

38. Mike Gray, *Drug Crazy: How We Got Into This Mess and How We Can Get Out* (New York: Random House, 1998), chapter 10. See also Richard Davenport-Hines, *The Pursuit of Oblivion: A Global History of Narcotics* (New York: W. W. Norton, 2002) and Joshua Wolf Shank, "America's Altered States: When Does Legal Relief of Pain Become Illegal Pursuit?" *Harper's* (May 1999). For a disturbing account of unexamined assumptions in our attitude toward mind-altering substances, see Daniel Pinchbeck, *Breaking Open the Head: A Psychedelic Journey into the Heart of Contemporary Shamanism* (New York: Broadway, 2002).

39. Ann Marlowe, *How to Stop Time: Heroin from A to Z* (New York: Anchor Books, 2000), 180.

40. Theodore Roszak, *The Making of a Counter Culture: Reflections on the Technocratic Society and Its Youthful Opposition* (New York: Anchor Books, 1969), 5.

41. See Steven Levenkron, *Cutting: Understanding and Overcoming Self-Mutilation* (New York: W. W. Norton, 1998). See also Caroline Kettlewell, *Skin Game: A Cutter's Memoir* (New York: St. Martin's, 1999) and Armando R. Favazza, *Bodies Under Siege: Self-Mutilation and Body Modification in Culture and Psychiatry* (Baltimore: Johns Hopkins University Press, 1996).

42. See Eric Fuchs, *Sexual Desire and Love: Origins and History of the Christian Ethic of Sexuality and Marriage,* Marsha Daigle, trans. (New York: Seabury Press, 1983), 142–43.

Chapter Four: Protecting Us from Ourselves

1. Lewis I. Bredvold and Ralph G. Ross, eds., *The Philosophy of Edmund Burke: A Selection from His Speeches and Writings* (Ann Arbor: University of Michigan Press, 1983), 44.

2. Ralph Waldo Emerson, "Circles," in *Essays: First and Second Series* (New York: Vintage / Library of America, 1990), 184. The paradox is that forgetting ourselves, leaping away, helps us find ourselves.

3. *The Consolation of Philosophy,* trans. Richard Green (Indianapolis: Bobbs-Merrill, 1962), 69.

4. John J. O'Connor, "Life After Drag: Unreality Endures," *New York Times,* 9 July 1996, C4.

5. See "Middle-Aged Fitness Freaks Dropping Like Stone," *New York Post,* 26 November 2001, 8. Research at Ohio State University showed a 200 percent increase in serious exercise-related incidents among men and women in their forties over the past twenty years.

6. *Princeton University Handbook,* 1999–2000 (on-line version). Among the many media references to the Nude Olympics, see "Princeton's Nude Run is Undone by the Weather," *New York Times,* 23 March 1998, A38, and "Naked Rite of Passage Defended at Princeton," *New York Times,* 5 March 1999, B5.

7. See the full text of the letter at http://www.umich.edu/fflurecord/0001/Apr09_01/5.htm.

8. Joseph Glenmullen, *Prozac Backlash: Overcoming the Dangers of Prozac, Zoloft, Paxil, and Antidepressants with Safe, Effective Alternatives* (New York: Simon & Schuster, 2000).

9. Norbert Elias, *The Civilizing Process: The Development of Manners,* Edmund Jephcott, trans. (New York: Urizen Books, 1978), 164.

10. Neil MacFarquhar, "Naked Dorm? That Wasn't in the Brochure," *New York Times,* 18 March 2000, A1.

11. Bertrand Russell, "In Defense of Idleness." Quoted in James Gleick, *Faster: The Acceleration of Just About Everything* (New York: Pantheon, 2000), 203–4.

12. Janice Dickinson, *No Lifeguard on Duty: The Accidental Life of the World's First Supermodel* (New York: Regan Books, 2002).

13. See Adam Liptak, "Internet Battle Raises Questions About Privacy and the First Amendment," *New York Times,* 2 June 2003, A13 (with photo); and Adam Liptak, "Florida to End Privacy Suit," *New York Times,* 23 July 2003, A15.

14. Sir Patrick Devlin, "The Enforcement of Morals," in S. Kadish and M. Paulsen, eds., *Criminal Law and Its Processes: Cases and Materials,* 3rd ed. (Boston: Little, Brown & Company, 1975).

Chapter Five: Self-Control

1. Ian McEwan, *Atonement* (New York: Anchor Books, 2003).

2. Zbigniew Brzezinski, *Out of Control: Global Turmoil on the Eve of the Twenty-First Century* (New York: Macmillan, 1993), x.

3. Peter Handke and Wim Wenders, *Les Ailes du Désir,* Dominique Petit and Bernard Eisencshitz, trans. (Le Chesnay: Jade-Flammarion, 1987), 164–67. For an English translation, see *Wings of Desire* (New York: Orion Home Video, 1989).

4. John Todd, *The Young Man: Hints Addressed to the Young Men of the United States* (Northampton, Mass.: J.H. Butler, 1845), 368. Quoted in Jeffrey P. Moran, *Teaching Sex: The Shaping of Adolescence in the 20th Century* (Cambridge, Mass.: Harvard University Press, 2000), 7. This section comes from Moran.

5. Andrew Sullivan, "Why Men Are Different: The Defining Power of Testosterone," *New York Times Magazine,* 2 April 2000, 48.

6. See Peter Gardella, *Innocent Ecstasy: How Christianity Gave America an Ethic of Sexual Pleasure* (New York: Oxford University Press, 1985), 60. See also G. J. Barker-Benfield, *The Horrors of the Half-Known Life* (New York:

Harper & Row, 1976), 130–32; Barbara Ehrenreich and Deirdre English, *For Her Own Good: 150 Years of the Experts' Advice to Women* (Garden City, N.Y.: Doubleday, 1978), 123; and Natalie Angier, *Woman: An Intimate Geography* (Boston: Houghton Mifflin, 1999), 76–81.

7. Cathleen Medwick, *Teresa of Avila: The Progress of a Soul* (New York: Knopf, 1999), 46.

8. Jeffrey Rosen, *The Unwanted Gaze: The Destruction of Privacy in America* (New York: Random House, 2000), 10.

9. Immanuel Kant, *Critique of Judgment*, trans. Werner S. Pluhar (Indianapolis: Hackett, 1987), 120.

10. Choderlos De Laclos, *Les Liaisons Dangereuses* (Paris: Flammarion, 1982), 172. The translation is my own.

11. Anne Edwards, *Throne of Gold: The Lives of the Aga Khans* (London: HarperCollins, 1995), 175.

12. Bertrand Russell, "The Sense of Sin," from Louis Greenspan and Stefan Andersson, eds., *Russell on Religion: Selections from the Writings of Bertrand Russell* (New York: Routledge, 2000), 190.

13. Evelyn Waugh, *Brideshead Revisited* (Boston: Little, Brown & Co., 1973), 230.

14. Rachel P. Maines, *The Technology of Orgasm* (Baltimore: Johns Hopkins University Press, 1999), x.

15. See David Sonstroem, "Teeth in Victorian Art," in *Victorian Literature and Culture*, vol. 29, no. 2 (2001): 351–82.

16. Lori Gottlieb, *Stick Figure: A Diary of My Former Self* (New York: Simon & Schuster, 2000).

17. Lisa Palac, *The Edge of the Bed: How Dirty Pictures Changed My Life* (Boston: Little, Brown & Co., 1998).

Chapter Six: The Men of UVa

1. On July 18, 2002, *The Hook*, a weekly paper published free for the residents of Charlottesville, Virginia, featured a lengthy interview with B., who referred readers to his Web site. B. did not reveal his name in the interview, although he was still familiar to many UVa students who no doubt read the interview and saw the accompanying pictures. Instead, B. went by his *nom de porn* "DC Chandler." See Courteney Stuart, "Hard at Work: Former Wahoo Hits Porn Bigtime" at www.readthehook.com.

2. Agnieszka Holland, *Europa, Europa* (Orion Home Video, 1992).

3. "Georgia: Conviction Under New Hate Crimes Law," *New York Times*, 12 June 2003, A33. Note that Price was ultimately acquitted of the hate crime charge, which would have brought five more years.

4. See Marcia Chambers, "Secret Videotapes Unnerve Athletes," *New York Times*, 9 August 1999, D4; and Jere Longman, "Videotaped Athletes Victorious in Court," *New York Times*, 5 December 2002, D8.

5. Meanwhile, mainstream American advertising for products like clothing and shoes increasingly leans on norms developed in the hugely profitable pornography industry. Indeed, actors from porn films are crossing into mainstream advertisements, with some success. See Stuart Elliott, "Pony Adds to Its Maverick Image," *New York Times*, 24 February 2003, C9.

6. Sandra Cisneros, "Guadalupe the Sex Goddess," in *Resurrecting Grace: Remembering Catholic Childhoods*, Marilyn Sewell, ed. (Boston: Beacon Press, 2001), 158.

7. For a rare account of how American women behave in restrooms, see Libby Copeland, "Instant Intimate: The Lady of the Ladies' Room," *Washington Post*, 27 April 2003, D1. For a fascinating window onto how women purchase bras, we have a *New York Times* obituary to thank (Douglas Martin, "Selma Koch, ninety-five, Famed Brassiere Maven" [14 June 2003, A16]). Few American men, it seems safe to say, would patronize a shop owner who made it his business to guess their intimate measurements. (The analogy is limited in so far as comparing breasts, the outlines of which are almost always visible, to penises, the outlines of which usually are not, might be like comparing apples to oranges.) Selma Koch died in New York City in June 2003 at the age of 95, after having achieved local fame for her ability to size up women at first glance. Many American women, it seems, wear an incorrect bra size. With just a single look, Koch could guess the appropriate size and quickly prove it with a private fitting.

8. Elisabeth Eaves, *Bare: On Women, Dancing, Sex, and Power* (New York: Knopf, 2002), 55.

9. Leo Steinberg, *The Sexuality of Christ in Renaissance Art and in Modern Oblivion* (Chicago: University of Chicago Press, 1996), 24, 36, 41.

10. Sigmund Freud, *Civilization and Its Discontents*, trans. James Strachey (New York: W. W. Norton, 1961), 34.

11. C. David Heymann, *RFK: A Candid Biography of Robert F. Kennedy* (New York: Dutton, 1998), 252. Tradition takes curious paths, for it seems that

some of our forebears associated a large penis with plebeians, even the devil. Satan, for example, was rumored in early modern Europe to have "a penis of monstrously bestial dimensions." See Stuart Walton, *Out of It: A Cultural History of Intoxication* (London: Hamish Hamilton, 2000), 60. And Thomas Laqueur marshals evidence that ancient Greeks prided themselves on having small penises, which they took as a biological sign of their social superiority. See *Making Sex: Body and Gender from the Greeks to Freud* (Cambridge, Mass.: Harvard University Press, 1992), 31–32.

12. Stephanie Mansfield, *The Richest Girl in the World: The Extravagant Life and Fast Times of Doris Duke* (New York: Putnam, 1992), 183. Two pages later, Mansfield reports that "Rubi" was once described as "eleven inches long and thick as a beer can."

13. Elisabeth Young-Bruehl, *The Anatomy of Prejudices* (Cambridge, Mass.: Harvard University Press, 1996), 3–4.

14. Douglas Sadownick, *Sex Between Men: An Intimate History of the Sex Lives of Gay Men Postwar to Present* (San Francisco: HarperCollins, 1996), 98.

15. John Munder Ross, *The Sadomasochism of Everyday Life: Why We Hurt Ourselves, and Others, and How to Stop It* (New York: Simon & Schuster, 1997), 34.

16. *Winkelmann von Goethe* (Zürich, 1943), 91, 92. Quoted in George Mosse, *The Image of Man: The Creation of Modern Masculinity* (New York: Oxford University Press, 1996), 67.

17. Charles Strawson, *Haunts of the Black Masseur: The Swimmer as Hero* (New York: Pantheon, 1992), 209.

18. In this regard, school policy mirrored military policy. For a polemical account of how gay men disrupt esprit de corps in military showers, see Paula Cameron, Kirk Cameron, and Kay Proctor, "Homosexuals in the Armed Forces," *Psychological Reports* 62 (1988), 211–19. About three-quarters of their sample reported unease at being naked around homosexuals.

19. Dick Johnson, "Students Still Sweat, They Just Don't Shower," *New York Times,* 22 April 1996, A1.

20. J. D. Rosenberg, *The Darkening Glass: A Portrait of Ruskin's Genius* (London: Routledge, 1963), 20.

21. Willard Gaylin, *The Male Ego* (New York: Viking, 1992), 78–79.

22. David Leavitt, *Arkansas: Three Novellas* (Boston: Houghton Mifflin, 1997), 51.

Chapter Seven: Beyond Our Control

1. See Jeffrey Zaslow, "Medical Mystery: Why Some Children Keep Setting Fires," *Wall Street Journal*, 27 June 2003, A1, A8.

2. Michael R. Gottfredson and Travis Hirschi, *A General Theory of Crime* (Stanford: Stanford University Press, 1990), 89–91.

3. Lisa Palac, *The Edge of the Bed*, 19–20.

4. Elinor Burkett and Frank Bruni, *A Gospel of Shame: Children, Sexual Abuse, and the Catholic Church* (New York: Viking, 1993), 94–95.

5. Kay Redfield Jamison, *Night Falls Fast: Understanding Suicide* (New York: Knopf, 1999), 196–97.

6. This information comes from Kay Redfield Jamison, *Night Falls Fast*, 172–73.

7. Peter Kramer, *Listening to Prozac* (New York: Penguin, 1997).

8. Matt Ridley, *Genome: The Autobiography of a Species in 23 Chapters* (New York: HarperCollins, 1999), 147–60.

9. David Sedaris, *Naked* (Boston: Little, Brown & Co., 1997), 7–9.

10. Andrew Solomon, "Anatomy of Melancholy," *The New Yorker*, 12 January 1998, 46–57. The article became the cornerstone for his book *The Noonday Demon* (New York: Scribner, 2001), perhaps the definitive study of depression.

11. Marie-Hélène Huet, *Monstrous Imagination* (Cambridge, Mass.: Harvard University Press, 1993).

12. "Repression." In *The Standard Edition of the Complete Psychological Works of Sigmund Freud*, J. Strachey, ed. and trans. (London: Hogarth Press, 1953–74), vol. 14, 143–58. Original work published 1915.

13. Quoted in Gamson, *Freaks Talk Back*, 9.

14. Dan Wegner, *White Bears and Other Unwanted Thoughts* (New York: Viking, 1989). See also D. M. Wegner, "You Can't Always Think What You Want: Problems in the Suppression of Unwanted Thoughts," in M. Zanna, ed., *Advances in Experimental Social Psychology* (vol. 25) (San Diego: Academic Press, 1992); and D. M. Wegner and R. Erber, "The Hyperaccessiblity of Suppressed Thoughts," *Journal of Personality and Social Psychology*, 63 (1992), 903–12.

15. Quoted in Edmund White, *Marcel Proust* (New York: Viking Penguin, 1999), 41–2, 107–8.

16. This is taken from Roger Shattuck, *Proust's Way: A Field Guide to "In Search of Lost Time"* (New York: W. W. Norton, 2000), 111–12.

17. Sigmund Freud, "Creative Writers and Day-Dreaming," *The Standard Edition of the Complete Psychological Works of Sigmund Freud,* vol. 9, 146.

18. Jerome Singer, *The Inner World of Daydreaming* (New York: Random House, 1966), 154.

Chapter Eight: Raving

1. For an absorbing account of how Turkish authorities have reacted to the hunger strikes of young, dissident students, see Scott Anderson, "The Hunger Warriors," *New York Times Magazine,* 21 October 2001, 43. Anderson detailed the longest and deadliest hunger strike against a government in modern history.

2. James Dao, "Navy Doctors Force-Feeding Two Prisoners," *New York Times,* 1 April 2002, A12. In early 2003, the Illinois Appellate Court, 4th District, ruled that a prison inmate on hunger strike must be force-fed and that such orders do not violate an inmate's constitutional right to privacy. See the *Chicago Daily Law Bulletin,* 17 January 2003 and 12 February 2003.

3. See Sarah Lyall, "Britain: Stitches Out," *New York Times,* 31 May 2003, A5 (with photo). Lyall's earlier article provided more details: "A Hunger Strike Puts Spotlight on British Asylum Policy," *New York Times,* 29 May 2003, A3.

4. *Washington Post,* "Crime and Justice," 11 July 2002, B2.

5. Christian Swezey, "Johnson, Virginia Are Left Standing," *Washington Post,* 27 May 2003, D1, D2.

6. Jean-Jacques Rousseau, "Discourse on the Origin and Foundations of Inequality Among Mankind," in *The Social Contract and The First and Second Discourses,* Susan Dunn, ed., Lester Crocker, trans. (New Haven: Yale University Press, 2002).

7. T. M. Luhrmann, *Of Two Minds: An Anthropologist Looks at American Psychiatry* (New York: Vintage, 2001), 144.

Chapter Nine: The Whole World's Gone Mad

1. John McWhorter, *Losing the Race: Self-Sabotage in Black America* (New York: Free Press), 2000.

2. Edward W. Said, "When will we resist? The U.S. is preparing to attack the

Arab world, while the Arabs whimper in submission," *The Guardian*, 25 January 2003, 22.

3. Dorothy Rabinowitz, *No Crueller Tyrannies: Accusation, False Witness, and Other Terrors of Our Times* (New York: Free Press, 2003). The film *Capturing the Friedmans* (New York: HBO Documentary Films, 2003) dreadfully illustrates the cost of the 1980s' child molestation witch hunt.

4. Juliet B. Schor, *The Overspent American: Upscaling, Downshifting, and the New Consumer* (New York: Basic Books, 1999).

5. Robert H. Frank, *Luxury Fever: Why Money Fails to Satisfy in an Era of Excess* (New York: Free Press, 1999), 3–4.

6. Thomas Sowell, *The Quest for Cosmic Justice* (New York: Free Press, 1999), 60. I follow Sowell closely in this section.

7. Eugene Ionesco, *Present Past, Past Present: A Personal Memoir* (1941), Helen R. Lane, trans. (New York: Grove, 1971), 30.

8. Arthur Schopenhauer, *The World as Will and Representation*, trans. E. F. J. Payne (New York: Dover, 1969), vol. I, 307.

Absent without Leave

1. Charles Taylor, *Sources of the Self: The Making of Modern Identity* (Cambridge, Mass.: Harvard University Press, 1989), 27.

index